DIGITAL
ARCHITECTURE
PASSAGES THROUGH HINTERLANDS

London Digital Diversity

It is a pleasure to write the forward for this publication. Why London? Why draw a conceptual line around London? Well, London, in contrast to other digital architecture hotspots, sports a diversity of architects and designers who are exploring and experimenting with a wider spectrum of practice paradigms. This diversity includes analogue / digital fabrication techniques, skin topologies, parametric urbanism, interactive systems, open-ended systems, some artisans are breathing life back into cybernetic ways of perceiving the world as performative and full of feedback loops. Others, such as myself, see parallels with surrealist protocols of space making within the new technologies. This is all how it should be—no overriding dogma. Yet it seems with the loss of dogma we have lost a sense of self-criticism and a sense of intellectual rigour that would hone our art more finely. So if these few words and the book generally is a snapshot in time, let it be the sort of snapshot in time that *Transarchitecture* (Paris 1998) embodied, a meeting of the cyber-tribes that had ramifications around the world. But let this book also be a plea for difference, not ubiquity of style, of surface or of ideology, but a revelling in the particular, the exceptional and reflect a delight in architecture and its discourses.

This would surely make those wonderful London-based pioneers of digital architecture proud of us. Cedric Price, Gordon Pask, John Frazer—look what you have done. We salute you and thank you for your vision!

As you know from engaging in the 'digital world', this publication is local and global simultaneously. It is a message in a bottle to our friends worldwide—transmitted around the world in a matter of seconds. I wish this book well as we set it adrift towards many stormy ports in a fast changing world. Now is not the time for formalist complacency, nor defunct doctrines or disembodied biomimicry. Chemical computing and nanotechnology is the new frontier, watch this space…

Neil Spiller is Professor of Architecture and Digital Theory and Vice Dean at the Bartlett, University College London

Half a century ago, Architect John Frazer shared a computer at Cambridge with John Conway, a prolific mathematician furthering the work of von Neumann's 'Cellular Automaton' and Turing's universal machines. In London, the Architectural Association of the early 60s was buzzing with technological optimism. Cedric Price and Gordon Pask discussed cybernetic systems to bring alive the visionary 'Fun Palace', while Archigram printed their pamphlets full of the promises of computation, communication and participatory culture. Strange hinterlands were envisaged, through which walking cities would trample, balloons would roam, buildings reconfigure at a whim and nomads plug in and plug out.

In the decades that followed, aeronautical and automotive industries drove the development of computer-aided design and manufacture, while simulation software inspired consensual hallucinations for cyber-architects to traverse. Finally, in the 1990s, the latent potential of the computer to augment practice spread through the work of Frank Gehry, Greg Lynn, and Mark Burry, to name but a few.

Over the past decade, the practice of architecture has radically transformed through the digital acceleration and sharpening of production. No office has been left untouched by the digital revolution—perhaps a cliché, since the digital is not special, nor remarkable. It is the norm, the invisible, the ubiquitous layer threaded through everything. As urban computing theorist Adam Greenfield proclaims, software and hardware has become 'every-ware'.

So why title a book 'Digital Architecture'? Is it perhaps a term such as 'horseless carriage', which will soon seem embarrassingly dated? The subject itself is a moving target, attempting to keep pace with the accelerating technological innovation enabled by computation.

Just as the architects of the mid-90s, inspired by the birth of the Internet, explored simulation, hyper surfaces and cyberspace,

INTRODUCTION

RUAIRI
GLYNN
SARA SHAFIEI

today an ever-expanding digital world is bifurcating new architectural agendas, processes and outcomes. Cloud computing, peer-to-peer and social networking, open source and creative commons have inspired participatory practices and design agendas resonating with the aspirations of Contant's 'New Babylon' and Friedman's 'Spatial City'.

Demystifying a world that has long been the domain of computer science, online communities share digital resources, radically lowering financial and knowledge base obstacles for a new generation of architects to become 'hackers' for the first time. Globally, young and highly skilled architects are transforming the industry.

Computation has meanwhile cracked the code of the human genome and our bodies are being explored at ever-increasing resolutions. Digital data is abundant, overflowing into our streets, our homes and our way of thinking. In architectural design our understanding of computation is shifting from binary ones and zeros, to encompass the performance of material and form. We can observe it in the skin of the soap bubble, the ear of a bat and the neural pathways of our brain. The digital has helped us understand the analog breathing architecture of our bodies and ecologies, inspiring a host of biomimetic and biotechnological opportunities, fundamentally changing the way we understand and design both form and behaviour.

Peter Cook colourfully described London's architecture scene as having Englishmen too often "trying to be as cool as the Swiss, as coy as the Dutch and as straightforward as the Americans". For half a century, away from the polite modernism of the larger London scene, a few schools and visionary architects have made London a leader in the theoretical and technical developments of an architecture that embraces digital speculation and conjecture.

The work in this book is neither conclusive nor shows allegiance to any specific aesthetic or otherwise agenda. Instead, it embraces the fervent energy found on the edges of architecture's hinterlands and takes a snapshot of London's latest, provocative projects from young graduates and practices. Oscillating between the analog and the digital, from concept to realisation, this book maps process and explores the diverse paths that lead to innovative spaces, poetic narratives and social interactions.

Matthew Shaw
Subverting the Lidar Landscape.

KENNY KINUGASA-TSUI

PLANTMORPHIC VOID

Prelude: Mysteries Of The Void

The term 'void' has been widely used in architectural vocabulary, but its qualities have been under-investigated in the discourse of contemporary digital design exploration. Historically, the void acquired different meanings between western and eastern culture. Emptiness had a more positive meaning in the East than in the West. Fear of empty space is a western phobia, yet it seems that the void has hardly been studied in Europe or the States, and not much theory on void had been formulated. Western cultures, such as sciences and mathematics, have directed mainly towards matter and energy, and there has been a tendency to pay more attention to the material, touchable, visible and easily measurable phenomena. Our technological culture has an ongoing driving force in western cultures, and it is especially noticeable in our digital contemporaries.

Comparative Analysis

On close inspection, there are historical similarities when it comes to the concepts of spiritual or sacred spaces. Both eastern and western cultures create sublime experiences of a 'paradise' or 'heaven', which are invisible matters within an enclosed physical boundary (most noticeably in gardens, temples and basilicas).

Various building typologies utilised the term 'void' to describe certain qualities of emptiness. Many baroque churches have an intrinsic projective quality to which the overlapped geometries of three-dimensional ovals (together with their religious ornamentation and codes) create a mental experience for the viewer that surpasses beyond the physical shells of the buildings. In the past century, various modern and post-modern theories explored architecture in its constructed or deconstructed fragments; the methodology was an assemblage of masses and voids.

In contemporary computer-aided exploration, the void has been considered as an empty space, or pockets of spaces, within a linear dimension of complex fields and forces. In my view, our digital contemporaries have, unfortunately, reduced the qualities of the void into a polemical dualism— the void is always 'black or white', 'it is either a mass or it isn't'.

It is important to realise that, in order for an empty space to be considered as a void, the space must be relational to a bigger, multi-dimensional, environmental ecology of elemental values or qualities. For example, a typical office basement or hotel lobby, without being in or part of a spatial choreography of excess and loss, may not embody the qualities of a void. In order for something to feel like a 'lack' or 'excess', either physically or on an experiential level, its relational mass or other substances (physical or psychological) must co-exist. Additionally, the void has a multiplicity of organic qualities; it can morph, evolve and adapt.

Organisms In Excess :The Voids Within

In botanical sciences, plant anatomy reveals nature's ability to create reconfigurable internality on a cellular level that allows the relational organism to be symbiotically dependant on its environmental context and surrounding species for survival. In plant cells, the notions of voids and mass carry mysterious relationships where they are constantly flipping, pulsating and undergoing metamorphosis. Metaphorically, such blurring and convolution essence in nature's foliage can be compared with the complex continuums of our cultural and social values, such as lushness and excessiveness, or shortage and deficiency. The contemporary void in digital design is non-linear, hybridised in an ecology of elemental values and experiential qualities.

These could, perhaps, be informed by its close relationships with the concepts of luxurious, luxuriant and loss. 'Luxurious' once had a close association with 'elegance' in the historical architectural discourse. This was most notable in the Baroque arts, where dramatic styles of form, geometries, tectonics, lavish foliage and ornamentation were intended to impress in the most sensual and opulent manner. In recent digital exploration, 'elegance' has been described as mediating and enabling complexity achieved by highly developed design ability. It also signifies a lightness of sophisticated structures that 'seemingly defy gravity'.[1] In the developments of current computer-driven design and manufacturing technologies, it is worth noting that a sophisticatedly designed complex form or structure (including high CADCAAM ornamentation) no longer carries the same luxurious values. What contemporary factors could re-inform, re-invigorate, re-define and re-design the once glorified conception of a luxurious experience?

'Luxuriance' is often confused with 'luxurious'. While its lush, thick, rich and exuberant qualities may be associated with luxury subjects, it can also be separated and identified as composite values of overindulgence, extravagance

plan 1:150

1330 sun axis

section 1:150

2007 A.D.

1200 A.D.

800 A.D.

100 A.D.

> A drawing of the main
void showing post-parametric
geometries of sacred spaces,
religious decorative patterns
and figural ornaments. The
veil skins become landscapes
that exfoliate, breathe,
sweat and bleed, feeding
the appetite for miracles,
prophecies and apparitions.

Voided Veilism

Lobby of Pilgrimage Hotel,
Rome.
Beatific Confessional lobby void
revealed by the flagellated veils,
symbolized by the foliage of The
Holy Tree.

> The proposed Pilgrimage
hotel is surgically inserted into
the original basilica, and acts
as a vertical intervention into
the historical archaeological
strata. Hence, the old and
new voids are intertwined for
confessional activities.

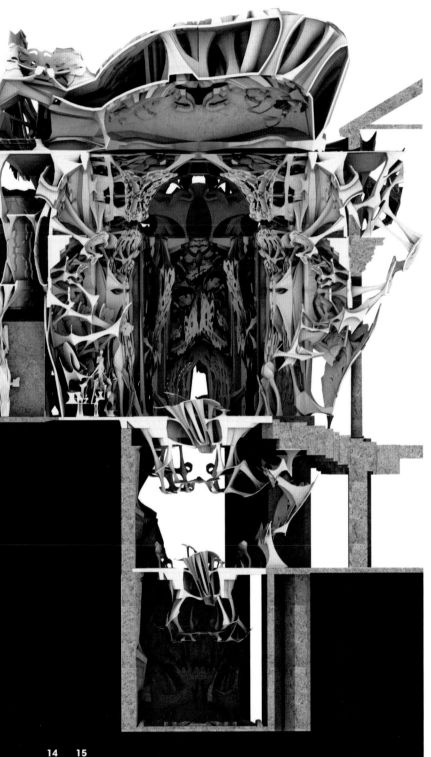

and superfluousness. For example, the 'luxuriant foliage' would be understood as a dark forest of rich and profuse growth. Such a characteristic in the natural wilderness could be compared with the growing chaos and complexity of modern day metropolis cities. The phenomena of 21st century consumer-driven culture is one that is excessive with lavish goods motivated by desires, sins and obsessions. Medieval construction was a primitive creation of boundaries to separate and protect man from harmful creatures in the wilderness; the enclosed space was a garden of paradise and safety. If our contemporary urban complexity carries the complex essence of a natural wilderness, what would it mean to construct and design the new urban garden?

'Loss', in architectural terms, has often been reduced to its lowest form—a negative matter emptied from a positive mass (for example, to Boolean, to subtract) or a deliberate creation of an empty space in a building (for example, lobby void, atrium void). However, it is important to recognise the deeper levels of loss as an embodied spatial experience filled with emotions. a phenomenological level of understanding requires a spatial and formal 'build up' of fragmented constructions of relational characteristics. In order to achieve the experience of loss, a void must be created within an ecological system of valuable substances. The void must be discovered; it is concealed within the illusions created by complex or excessive foliage that requires exploration and navigation. The foliage could be defined as natural, artificial or semi-living material. Examples could be found in many historical gardens in Kyoto, Japan, where the essence of the void / loss was carefully crafted and inserted into a complex composition of sculptural wooden roofs, pavilions arrangements, layered corridors, manipulated plant growths, water circulation, exterior or internal landscaping and structural preservation. The talented ancient Japanese gardener was multi-skilled in archaeology, botany and architecture designing spaces that would evoke the sublime, the blissful and the mysterious.

Consequently, luxurious, luxuriance and loss create qualities of illusion to conceal the voids within; this can be compared to the concepts of exuberant fluidity and illusions during the Baroque. The progressive continuum (and morphing) of luxurious, luxuriance and loss, therefore, make up the values and elements of the contemporary urban foliage. This creates an ecology within which the notions of voids can mediate. Such embodiment is an architectural methodology that nurtures a necessary sensibility towards the site and context, in prehistory and history, as well as their futuristic design potential. The hybridised theoretical approach can be compared to the working methods of an archaeologist and a botanist in terms of recovery, documentation, analysis and interpretation of material remains, such as cultural codes and environmental data (including artefacts, biofacts, and topographical data). Altogether, the 'void methodology' rejuvenates an intertextual understanding, driven by human curiosity to discover mysterious values of space and place. Such emotional responses then become the ingredients for stimulating a narrative for new interventions. The following research project is experimental of such notions.

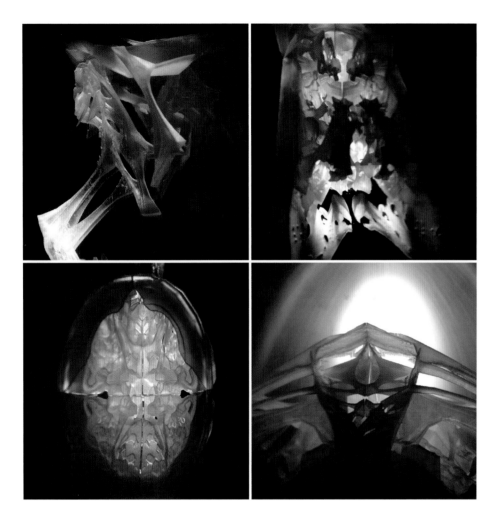

∧ A set of photographic analysis showing the tectonics of the veils undergoing bio-metaphoric projection, duplication, repetition, surface creation, and multiplication into layers of flesh skins to conceal three-dimensional interstitial volumes and voids.

∨ The monochromatic digitally prefabricated resin prototypes mimic natural charcoal, allowed to decay and deform, creating non-machine-like qualities, and the final void model.

> The curious exploration is enabled by the morphological foliage, which creates surface deformations from the external orthogonal basilica grid to the internal fluid dynamics.

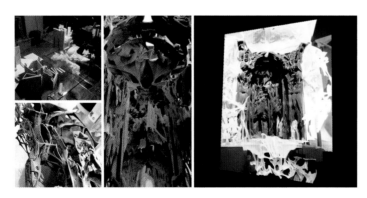

Voided Veilism

The Basilica of St Clemente in Rome is an archaeological site of mystic edifices. Evidence suggests a blissful mosaic depiction of the Bible myth, the Holy Tree of Life that once sanctified the underground spaces of the basilica. The symbolical foliage has been poetically interpreted as 'digital veils', of which their inherent particles contain pre-established information that could spark a projective construction system of divine architectural tectonics.

The veils would continue to project, duplicate, repeat and multiply into layers of interstitial boundaries to divide and create voids from mass. The projective system is composed of nodes of voids that generate expansion and compression fields and voids are used for public circulation and confessional uses. Similar to the behaviour of mass and voids in the anatomy of plant cells, these inhabitable voids are concealed and formed by layers of skins that would define their corporeal volumes. The directional forces of the veils' surface morphology generate an intuitive guidance route for circulation and exploration, leading to discovery on a choreographic journey.

The poetic experience of the voids is created by the illusionistic qualities of excessiveness, lavishness, extravagance, exuberance and lushness. The proposed pilgrimage hotel reinvigorates the original basilicas as a vertical intervention into the historical archaeological strata, wherein the morphological tectonics intertwine the old and the new voids for confession.

The project is beautifully represented through a series of digitally prefabricated drawings and prototype models involving the use of mirrors and directional stage lighting,. Manifested virtual images of the void spaces for the viewer allow the overall experience of the voids to be constructed by both physical and psychological means.

1. *Elegance (Architectural Design)* edited by Ali Rahim, Hina Jamelle, published by Academic Press 2007.

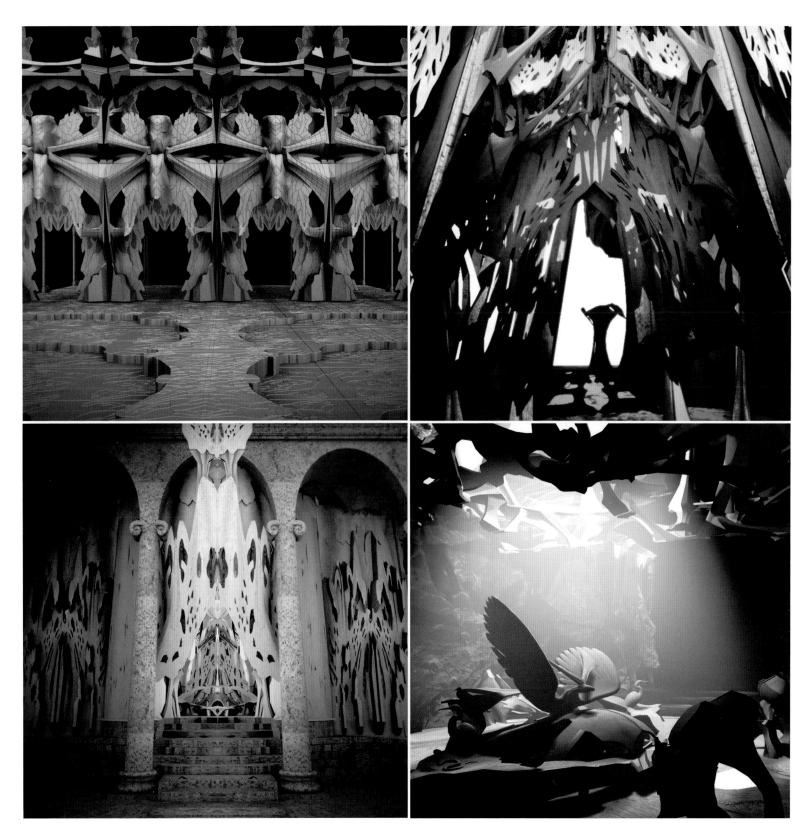

HQ FOR THE ORGANISATION OF ISLAMIC CONFERENCES (OIC) ISTANBUL

Istanbul is the only international metropolitan hub that embraces two continents, providing an extraordinarily complex cultural setting for Damjan Iliev's design for the Organisation for Islamic Conferences (OIC) Forum. Aimed at integrating Istanbul's rich historic past as a centre of trade and religion with its increasing importance in world-wide politics, the deigns examines optical defocus and cognitive illusions, using techniques of transparency and refraction, openness and veiling.

Studying human cognition, in particular the limitations of peripheral vision, the design process began with experiments to challenge preconceived notions of visual perception using methods of reflection, refraction and distortion. A series of laser-cut isomorphic models were constructed generating optical illusions based on projected geometries. These studies led to the investigation of specific panoramic vantage points within and around the Asian side of Istanbul. A mixed-use proposal (predominantly of the OIC as their permanent headquarters), the programme consists of a debating chamber, secretariat offices, assembly rooms, press centre and an exterior public amphitheatre. The façade interface represents the most intricate part of the scheme as it separates the private debating chamber from the public amphitheatre.

Employing an array of Fresnel lenses that obstruct clear visual penetration from the exterior, and simultaneously animate dispersed reflections from the activities within its immediate surrounding, the delegates within the debating chamber are separated from the outside world while being continuously reminded of it by the presence of the public.

Developed originally for lighthouses, Fresnel lenses enable the construction of large aperture lenses and short focal length without the weight and volume of material, which would be required in conventional lens design. The lenses can be used to make an image appear larger, smaller or distorted in a specified manner, or even displaced. Incoming light can also be dispersed or focused to a specific point or line.

Given the variable characteristics of the lenses, the façade system consists of several different Fresnel modules that fenestrate the entire surface achieving variable levels of visual permeability. Computer-controlled milling equipment (normally used during the manufacture of complex Fresnel lenses for lighthouses) could be transferred to the engineering and design of the interface façade. Different lens modules are made offsite and later delivered and installed.

The dialectic established between inside and out is envisioned as delivering appropriate working conditions with a sentiment of democracy and transparency within the workings of the OIC. Iliev describes his proposal as delivering, "an architectural and political statement without becoming monumental or overtly politically correct. It attempts to create a building that symbolises the OIC and its member states while simultaneously evading the traditionalist Islamic aesthetic". This, Illiev argues, has contributed to centuries of "cultural, religious and political disputes."

> Interior perspective.

- Preliminary facade studies into the nature of human vision, perspective distortion and visual permeability.

- Aerial view from nearby mosque —an attempt for a pan-Islamic architectural statement.

- Laser-cut isomorphic models create optical illusion that visually alternates from various points of view.

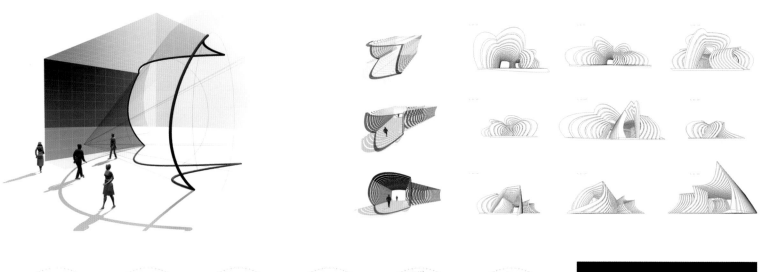

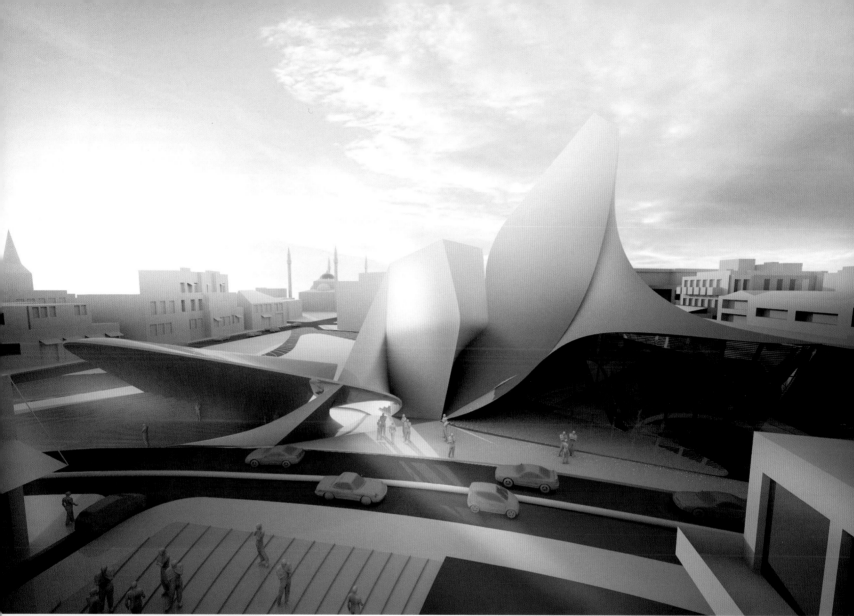

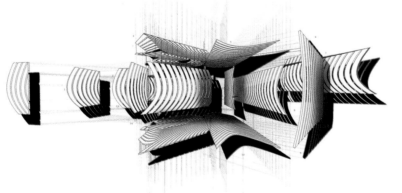

DAVID GREENE & SAMANTHA HARDINGHAM

RESEARCH BY DESIGN
WORKSHOP 01

PROFILE

Architect, educator and founding member of Archigram, David Greene has been hugely influential on generations of architects and designers through his iconic projects, such as Living Pod and Log Plug, and his ongoing inquisitive, oppositional approach to teaching. In 2002, Greene won the RIBA Annie Spink award in recognition of his outstanding contribution to architectural education. He continues to develop the 'Invisible University', with Samantha Hardingham, as a live research project at the Research Centre of Experimental Practice EXP at the University of Westminster.

A well-serviced primitive
explores the architecture
of the new nature.

Text and Images
Samantha Hardingham
and David Greene / The
Invisible University

Digital Photography
and Imagery
Kevin Shepherd and
Sara Shafiei

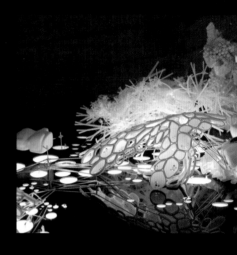

L.A.W.U.N.* PROJECT #20

(28th April–24th May 2008, Architectural Association)

In 2008, Greene, working in collaboration with Hardingham, invited a number of designers to revisit original projects, reviewing their context in relation to contemporary construction and digital techniques. Conceived as part of an ongoing workshop, these new commissions revisited four of Greene's original projects. The resulting exhibition (of the above title) and accompanying publication (L.A.W.u.N Project #19) explored Greene's interest in how new technologies inform new architectures by demonstrating increasing disinterest in form and a wilful drift towards invisibility.

Minimaforms was invited to rethink and evolve Greene's seminal project the Living Pod and High-Rise Tower. This incorporated the remaking of part of Greene's original High-Rise Pod model and new model that explored a metamorphosis of the original living pod/pod tower through a process that privileged evolutionary tactics through behavioural response as a stimulus for collective engagement. Pods evolve tails and communities form through animalistic tendencies. Units act as mirrors, observing, recording and broadcasting the occupational patterns as a form of emotive conditioning. The aim was to speculate on models that could engage man through feedback and circular activity and evolve new concepts of living through dynamic organisation and social experimentation.

Living Pod and High-Rise Tower workshop team: Theodore Spyropoulos, Stephen Spyropoulos, David Greene, Yoshimasa Hagiwara, Eleni Pavlidou, Shajay Bhooshan, Yasuhiro Tohdoh, Pierandrea Angius and Alkis Dikaios.

Artist and architect Shin Egashira worked on Greene's thesis project, a mosque for Baghdad (1958). Textile sculptor Rowan Mersh designed and made a prototype of the very first 'hairy coat' (see previous page), a manifestation of Greene's audio visual piece entitled 'The World's Last Hardware Event' (1967) that imagines a world where man can wander, carrying his architecture in his pocket (pre-empting the arrival of mobile phones and memory sticks). Filmmaker Nic Clear re-mixed a new version of a short film about Greene's 'Invisible University', containing footage edited by David Greene and Samantha Hardingham.

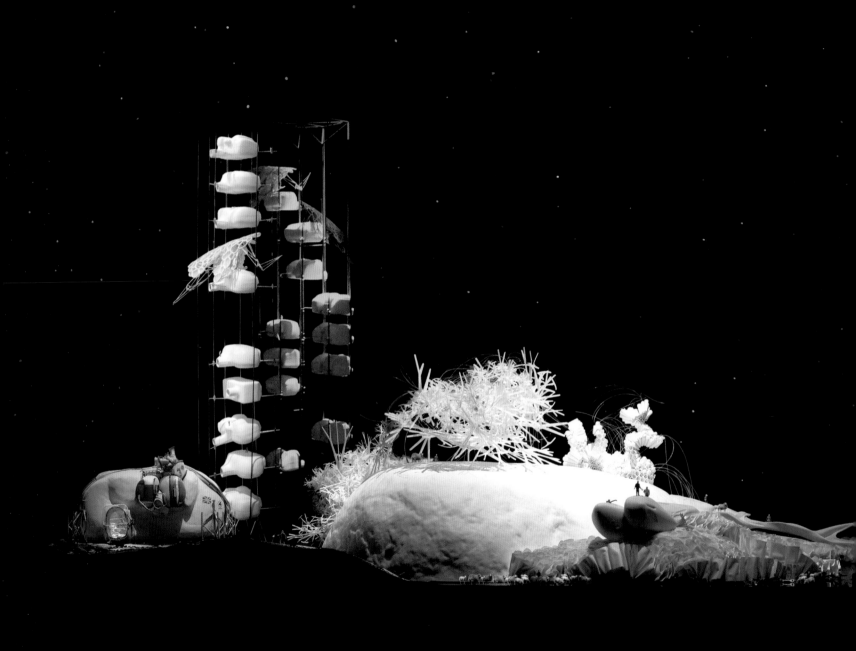

< Itinerant battery-powered
coastal terrain.

Stupefied by the micro-sequins
of a post-digital construction
site revisited, almost anything
that you can imagine is going
to happen. Radically altered
socio-cultural investigations into
conditions of an architecture
as a sensitive responsive
system, an electronic topology
constantly tuning and retuning
itself. The cool metallic scaffolds
move by toppling over (a very
reliable way to get around)
and crane armatures lean
into the lightness of night-time,
assembling and reassembling
a superbly eloquent but broken
architecture. Wrecked urbanity
upon wrecked urbanity, dainty
weeds, mouldering aqueducts
and unseen larks disturbing the
rumble of construction. The
scanty antiquarian remnants
move in a romantic reverie
towards a soft, placid, essentially
innocent present to the
peaceful bleating of sheep.

Notes
1 L.A.W.u.N (Locally Available
   World unseen Networks)
   Project #20 is made by IU
   faculty members: David
   Greene, Samantha
   Hardingham, Rowan Mersh,
   Theo Spyropoulos, Shin
   Egashira, Isabel Peripherique,
   Edwin Kendall, Kevin
   Shepherd and Sara Shafiei.
2 EW Manwaring, Italian
   Landscape in Eighteenth
   Century England, Cass
   (London), 1925

**Text and Images
Samantha Hardingham and
David Greene / The Invisible
University**

**Digital Photography
and Imagery
Kevin Shepherd
and Sara Shafiei**

MICHAEL WIHART

REMOTE PROSTHETICS:
IMPRESSIONS OF TRANSIENT PROXIMITIES

The 'Remote prosthetics: Impressions of transient proximities' project has been developed to reflect on human interaction with participatory architectural environments. The project anticipates a future where alternative environments are dynamically constructed by soft architectural machines, and where man's intervention in the world transcends the dichotomy of biological *versus* technological and natural *versus* man-made. The project proposes to use physical components described as soft- and wet-ware to guide the human use of architecture (the architectural use of man: to the same extent that we are using architecture, architecture is using us). In this world, the possibilities for exchange of delight and enjoyment between user and architecture take precedence over a utilitarian use of space. In conceiving a spatial environment that reconfigures over time, we have to look at means of introducing motional change as well as establishing means for the control for the responsive functioning of the system.

The project operates on the threshold between responsiveness and interaction, and while the object is a built artefact, it is also an erratic performer on the stages of our imagination. The subtitle, 'impressions of transient proximities', indicates that this project focuses on the temporal spatial relationships fundamental to how we understand and operate in our environment. Remote prosthetics are our symbolic architectural companions mediating between new conditions of closeness and severance. They are remote to our body, but they are intimately linked to our sentiment and well-being.

Protocols For Soft Machines
'Remote prosthetics' is an ecology of 'soft machines' and their doubles. Their protocols of guidance are palimpsests as they learn and reevaluate the various motives of our spatial coexistence. These soft machines utlise gravitational forces and pneumatic and hydraulic systems in order to inform their configuration and behaviour. These soft architectural machines are enquiring, not only into the causes of the movement of their own mechanism, but forcibly transferring with other soft machine assemblies in other positions, symbiotically and symbolically mimicking gestures of stability and movement.

A consequence of the decision to construct assemblies that can interact with each other and their

> Cybernetic circus — collection of erratic performers on the stage of the cybernetic memory theatre, left to right: cardan joint model, hairy microphones studies, soft machine dementia, peripheral vision montage of Rem Koolhaas in New York, bitumen chicken and snail's space snail space joint model.

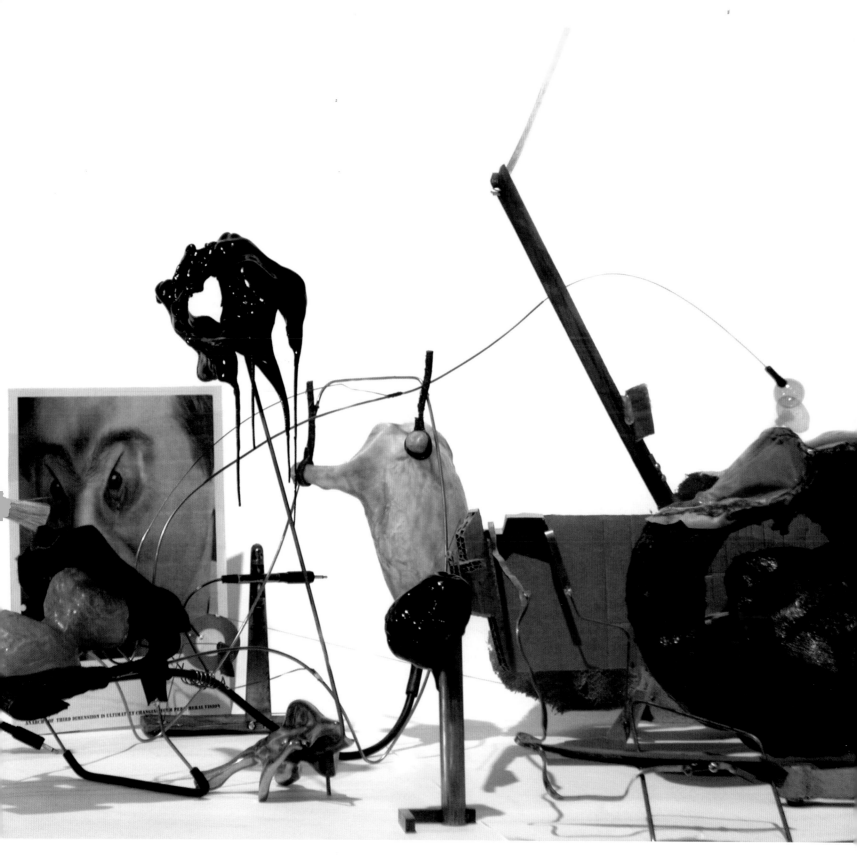

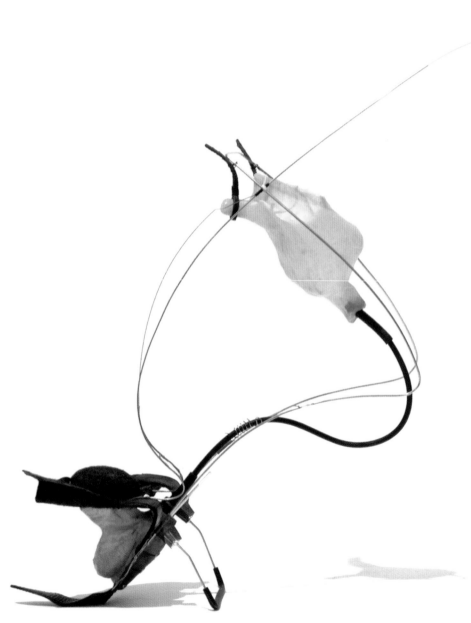

environment was to program, only to a certain extent, the possible actions of the assemblies and allow for a degree of elasticity that would make the resulting movements soft and slow. The effects of gravity, friction and inertia are integral to this design. The essential benefits are that softness and slowness can become the characteristics for the body and performance (*corpus* and *motus*) of such an assembly. This assembly cannot be defined as an operational machine that repeatedly fulfils a prescribed task. The motions of this soft device are sedate, clumsy and sometimes convulsive. Even though these motions are designed not to be predictable, they are functioning in an engineered framework that is derived from basic concepts in cybernetics. Its 'hairy microphones' (acoustic sensors) are attuned to the sound of movement in its proximity, while 'cardanic joints' (hydraulic actuators) are spatial operators constructing ephemeral sensations of slow space gestures.

The Construction Of Gestures
The chosen methods for the induction of movement are hydraulics and pneumatic mechanisms. They can operate as motional manipulators of the corpus of architecture. These systems enable flexible transmission of force through tubes, which affords great freedom of positioning and manoeuverability for the actuating mechanism in space. This enables the induction of spatial movement to be adjusted in spectrums of velocity and force.

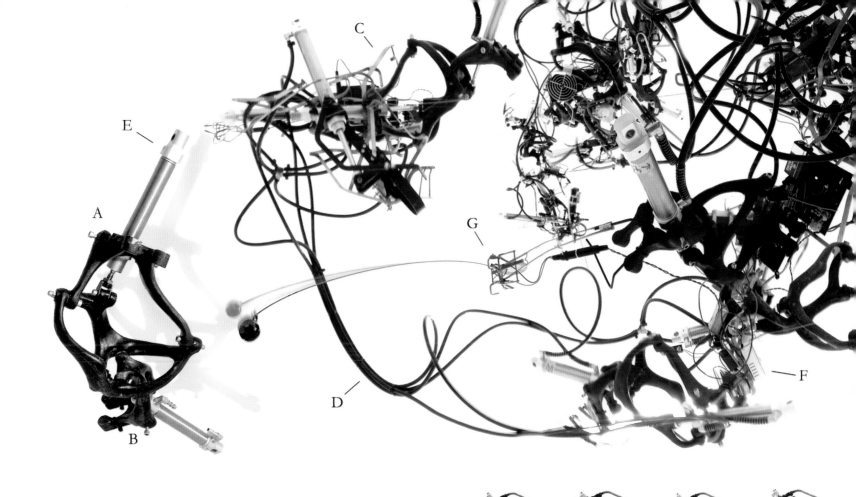

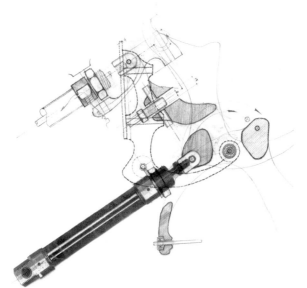

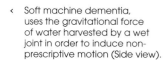

‹ Soft machine dementia,
 uses the gravitational force
 of water harvested by a wet
 joint in order to induce non-
 prescriptive motion (Side view).

⌃ Soft machines of Remote
 Prosthetics with Hairy
 microphones.

⌃› Cardanic joint with linear
 hydraulic actuators and its
 spatial movement.

› Construction drawing
 of cardanic joint for a
 soft machine.

The basic unit of a soft machine assembly is a cardanic joint, consisting of three articulate GRP (glass reinforced plastic) elements with embedded linear actuators. These pistons activate the cardanic joint in order to alter its position in space. A single joint is operated by two pistons, resulting in movement in two independent spatial axes, X and Y. A combination of multiple cardanic joints generates greater spatial occupation, while their gravitational pull exerts greater forces on other assemblies.

The cardanic joints (A and B) are mounted on a framework (C) and connected to each other with hydraulic tubes (D) in such a way that their own weight can reduce or increase the movement initially induced by the pistons (E). The tube and piston system is filled with hydraulic oil, but a buffer of air remains in each cylinder. Each soft machine has got one piston that is used as a pump. It is controlled by a processing unit (F) that digitally processes sound that is picked up by a series of sound sensitive devices (G), so called 'hairy microphones'.

> A drawing of the main
void showing post-parametric
geometries of sacred spaces,
religious decorative patterns
and figural ornaments. The
veil skins become landscapes
that exfoliate, breathe,
sweat and bleed, feeding
the appetite for miracles,
prophecies and apparitions.

NICHOLAS SZCZEPANIAK

A DEFENSIVE ARCHITECTURE

In a landscape plighted by climate change and rising water levels, social order breaks down, resources become rationed and public space becomes further militarised to maintain social order. Set in the Blackwater Estuary, Essex, Nick Szczepaniak's allegorical and provocative defensive architectures envisage the construction of a set of austere coastal defence towers that perform multiple functions within this dystopian future.

The militarised towers are alive—breathing, creaking, groaning, sweating and crying when stressed. Airbags on the face of the towers expand and contract, while hundreds of tensile trunks are sporadically activated, casting water onto the heated facades producing steam. An empty watchtower at the top of each tower gives the impression that the fragile landscape below is being constantly surveyed.

Across the estuary, a bed of salt marshes provides a natural flood defence and habitats for wildlife. Due to rising water levels and adverse weather conditions, the salt marshes are quickly deteriorating. The proposal suggests that mega structures can be integrated into, and encourage, the growth of natural defence mechanisms.

Over time, sand is collected at the base of each tower to form a spit across the mouth of the estuary, absorbing energy from the waves. Internally, the towers serve as a vast repository for mankind's most valuable asset—knowledge. The architecture is an ark, protecting books from cumulative and catastrophic deterioration.

Early experiments with sugar and caramel were used to develop a prototypical object that responds to its surrounding climate. A series of experiments with domestic objects demonstrated how molten caramel can be extruded in a state of tension, then left to set to act in compression. Thin sheets, up to one metre in height, were also formed and then hung as a curtain. Responding to environmental conditions, these objects would crack, split, absorb moisture and dilapidate. They became indicators of climate change and became beacons of abnormal environmental conditions.

Szczepaniak's project identified repetition, control, anticipated tension and surveying from an elevated position as properties crucial to his architecture. These evolved through an intensive process of speculative drawing, model making and a series of analogue and digital collage techniques. Studies were made of defensive typologies, in particular

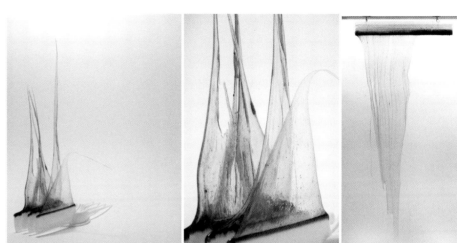

∧ Prototypical sugar curtain to one metre in height, then hung and left to respond to immediate climate.

< Ten Towers in context.

^ Tensile Trunks — facade detail
  in a state of anticipated tension.

^> Reading room chandelier
  development model —
  Bleeding light.

watchtowers and the Maze prison, built at the height of the Northern Irish Conflict.

The Maze prison is a model of repetitive and systematic architecture. Its primary function was to contain and isolate. Its geography is clear and functional, but also repetitive and confusing. Immediately inside the walls of the Maze is a 15 foot-wide void, known as inertia, which runs parallel to the wall and is divided into 36 stages. The primary function of inertia is to detect prisoners trying to escape and it can be considered a defensive strategy.

> View within Plaza Pool looking at the front of the Big Door.

Amanda Levete Architects' practice ethos is rooted in design research and a commitment to exploring the transformative potential of space. Developments in digital fabrication have allowed the office to challenge conventional notions of form and space alongside the continued value placed on hand-drawings and hand-crafted models. As an extension of its design research agenda, the office uses the design of furniture and objects to explore architectural ideas and test material possibilities at a smaller, more intimate scale and collaborates with materials manufacturers to push the boundaries of their fabrication techniques.

Amanda Levete, together with directors Alvin Huang, Kwamina Monney and Ho-Yin Ng, formed AL_A following the end of Levete's 20-year partnership with the late Jan Kaplicky at Future Systems.

One of the most innovative practices of its time, Future Systems completed award winning and internationally recognised buildings, including Selfridges department store in Birmingham and the media centre at Lord's cricket ground, which won the prestigious Stirling Prize.

AMA
LE
ARCHIT

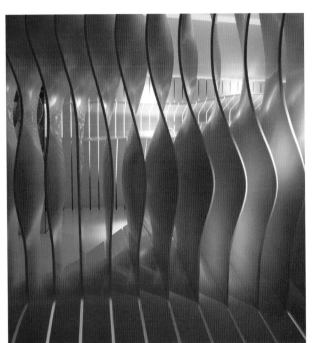

CORIAN LOUNGE

The lounge is a loosely defined architectural concept about a space that is animated by the movement of people in transit. A drop of water creating a series of ripples became the metaphor for transforming space through movement. The Corian lounge installation is about revealing the moment of change through visual complexity. The project pushes the technical possibilities of DuPont™ Corian® by exploiting its pliability and using the twisted geometry of the sheets to bring structural integrity. Advanced digital technology was used as part of the process for generating the design as well as for the fabrication of the installation. The lighting is designed to emphasise both the voids and the visual movement of the piece.

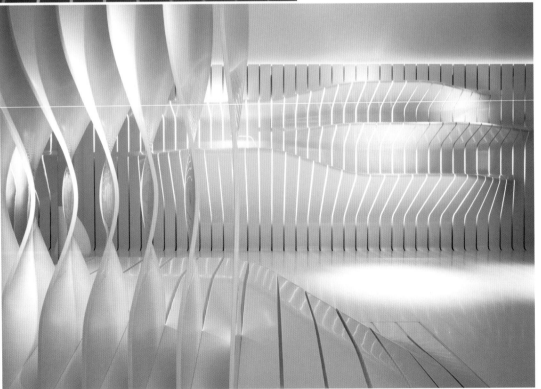

SPENCER DOCK BRIDGE

The 40 metre span bridge with its fluid lines and undulating concrete surface will take trams, traffic and pedestrians across the Royal Canal. The edges of the deck peel down to reveal a space for pedestrians to pause and take in views of the dock and Linear Park, which is currently under construction.

The underside of the bridge merges with the piers in a single movement with joint lines in the concrete designed to accentuate the geometry of the form. The finish of the concrete provides high visibility against the dark water of the canal and at night the structure will be vibrantly lit from below, giving the bridge a significant presence.

The proportions of the bridge are unusual and the design exploits this by treating the bridge as a piece of landscape design. The soft geometry and asymmetry of the design creates a piece of infrastructure that resolves the tension between form and function.

The bridge has been constructed from an innovative combination of insitu and precast reinforced concrete. The formwork for the sculpturally formed soffit was milled from high density expended polystyrene and coated in resin to achieve a smooth surface finish suitable for maritime environments. White limestone and cement was used in the concrete mix to achieve a white finish to give high visibility and reflect the pattern of the water. Milling directly from our 3D parametric models provided a high degree of control over the geometry. This innovative use of CNC cut polystyrene is to date the largest application of the material to be used in this way. The concrete edges were precast offsite and incorporate recessed lighting and the stainless steel balustrade.

Commissioned as Future Systems, the bridge is one of the first major projects completed under the name of Amanda Levete Architects. The bridge will be fully operational in 2010 to coincide with completion of the Linear Park.

Interview with Amanda Levete and Alvin Huang of AL_A

Q. How would you describe the emerging style of Amanda Levete Architects when compared with that of Future Systems? Can you describe the evolution in your work from your first projects to the present day?

AL: From a conceptual standpoint, our work remains rooted in the same experimental spirit embedded in the work we completed as Future Systems. As AL_A, we continue to foster that spirit with a desire to push boundaries through research-driven design methods that challenge convention. By merging diametrically opposed elements (physical and metaphysical, organic and man-made, digitally-generated and hand-crafted), we seek to enrich the built environment by creating the unexpected.

Q. Which other young architects' works do you find interesting?

AH: SHoP Architects, BIG, MAD, SPAN, IK Studio and theverymany.

Q. Do you seek inspiration from other disciplines?

AH: As the architectural profession has evolved, the buildings we design, the briefs we respond to and the cities we live in have all become far more complex. As a result, architects are finding they need to become more and more trans-disciplinary. Our inspirations come from a range of other disciplines, including biology, geology, physics, computation, mathematics, aeronautics, craft and art.

Q. What effect has digital technology had on the practices' ability to refine initial ideas off the page into fully developed building proposals?

AL: Digital technology has given us the ability to test, manipulate and refine ideas, and also challenge notions of space and development potential by exploring form and context in dynamic ways. But this technology is not an end in itself—without responsibility or editing, it becomes mannerist in the extreme. However, when exploited by architects with talent, who are in control of their tools, it is exciting beyond belief. It is perhaps ironic that something so profoundly technical has tipped the debate about ornament and structure, function and form, and frame and skin.

Q. At what stage do computers enter into the design process? Could you take us through your design approach on a particular project?

AH: We initiate exploration with 3D models and digital techniques from the outset of each design task. Computers have become an integral component in the design process itself, allowing us to generate, model and test iterative ideas with greater dexterity and increased accuracy. It is important to note, however, that the computer is not the key to the design process itself—our design concepts are the drivers. We value 3D models, hand drawings and physical models equally as the tools and techniques that enable our ideas.

On the Corian installation, we started with the client brief, which called for a conceptual airport lounge installation made entirely out of Corian. We quickly identified three driving concepts that ultimately shaped the entire project:

Be honest to the material and express the Corian sheets as a surface material, rather than as a homogenous solid (which is how Corian is often used);

Capitalise on the material performance of Corian and use thermoforming as a method to allow us to alter the shape and embed structural stiffness—we wanted to get maximum impact from the minimum amount of material;
Interpret the airport lounge as space of transition, where one is between modes of transit. This transition was made analogous to a drop of water in a pool of water—as the ripples expanded from the drop, we wanted to capture that moment in physical form; and,
Design not only the intellectual concept, but the method of making the installation.

We then began a parallel process of developing both our own design concept for the lounge and a variable moulding system for Corian (allowing us to fabricate from a single mould). We also conducted physical experiments on the material performance of thermo-formed Corian, while also rationalising the geometries we were producing to minimise wastage through the use of off-cuts.
The four parallel experiments created a continuous feedback loop where our aesthetic and intellectual decisions were also being driven by fabrication possibilities and material performance constraints. All of these experiments were facilitated by the fact that our fabricators

and installers all spoke the same three-dimensional language as we did. Designs were developed with parametric models, which were used to fabricate and mould physical prototypes to be tested. The results were used as constraints to re-define the parametric models. This cycle continued for a number of rapid iterations, which culminated with the installers using our 3D model on-site as an assembly guide.

In the end, we were able to produce a highly complex visual effect while remaining completely buildable. None of this would have been possible if all of the parties involved hadn't able to speak the same language.

Q. Your recent collaboration with DuPont on the Corian Super-Surfaces Installation is an example of architects and material engineers having a direct relationship with each other in the design and fabrication of architecture. How do you see the architectural profession evolving toward hybrid practices? Is this necessarily a good or bad thing?

AH: Architecture exists in three-dimensions. Building components are inherently three-dimensional. Yet, as a result of the industrial revolution and the introduction of standardisation, the procurement process of architecture has been reduced to the delivery of projected drawings as representations of design intent. We see digital technology as a return to a previous era, where the development of an idea was conceived, developed, analysed and even built from three-dimensional physical models. Digital technology is an enabler of a truly three-dimensional dialogue between designers, engineers, fabricators and installers. It serves as the medium for a continuous dialogue between the various parameters and constraints involved in the delivery of the project. We're not quite at the stage where we can fabricate a building, but we are clearly at a stage where building components are being fabricated directly from our digital files.

Q. AL_A share a revealing film of the digital processes behind the design of the Super-Surface. It's refreshingly open of you to do so when so many architects are secretive about the processes behind their work. Why have you chosen to do this?

AH: As architects and designers, we are just as interested in the process of designing and making things as in the results. Just as an inspiration image, concept sketch or study model sheds light on a project, we felt it was important to share the parametric control we achieved. There is an intellectual dialogue that surrounds every architectural project,

and we feel it is important to be able to connect our work to a broader architectural discourse.

Q. What advice would you offer young graduates today?

AL: There is a financial crisis, but there is not a creative crisis. It's an incredibly exciting moment, the moment to be bold, to think big and to think diagonally; because creativity goes hand-in-hand with entrepreneurship.

Q. What's next for your practice and the industry as a whole?

AL: The boundaries of an architect's role are becoming ever more blurred. Architects work in fashion, furniture, industrial design and curation, as well as good old-fashioned building. And more is being asked of them as thinkers and social commentators; although I think architecture has become less polemical than in the past. For the top 15% of architects, all this is empowering and enriching, but it is deeply marginalising to the other 85%, which you could argue is either good for quality or bad for the inevitability of artless buildings designed by default.

There is still the expectation that an architect is the creator of utopian space, which can be a bit limiting when what you want to do is push the boundaries of what is possible and take the public with you. Architecture, despite its necessity, is still an introspective endeavour. Debates and discussions are usually with like-minded groups using language that can, at times, be impenetrable, and it is only when there is controversy that the public becomes fully engaged. Until architecture and design are put on the educational curriculum, I suspect that this is the way it will remain.

The next 20 years will be pivotal. There is a real awareness of the power and fragility of our political, environmental and technological systems, and we have everything to play for. We owe it to ourselves and to future generations to do so to the best of our abilities.

JORDAN HODGSON

WORKHOUSE OF THE INFRASTRUCTURAL (COUNTER) REFORMATION

By 2032, the chaotic urban conditions that once helped define Elephant and Castle have given rise to a cripplingly disenfranchised underclass. In this bleak landscape of proletariat discontent, might the British government revert back to Victorian modes of jurisdiction, while simultaneously providing an architectural placebo to soothe a nervous population?

Unprecedented levels of unemployment following the crash of 2008, combined with a paralysis of social mobility, triggers the re-inauguration of the once proliferate workhouse typology. A re-branded Victorian-style workhouse, reminiscent of a lost empire, provides a sanctuary for adrift individuals and re-engenders the crucial workforce required for a British industrial renaissance. The lost industries of the golden age are reawakened from decades of inactivity and made manifest in a glorified cathedral for the plebeians of Elephant and Castle.

Car manufacturing and living quarters are positioned uncomfortably adjacent to bureaucratic authority, with a constitution of rational, efficiency and profit making engendered throughout. A sprawling workhouse, providing a clear separation between its occupants and the population of Elephant and Castle at large, gradually inhabits the infrastructurally intensified cityscape. A language of sublime ornamentation and excess pervades a sense of authoritative power over the workers, but a gain in momentum sees the emergence of an architectural encrustation that quite literally embodies the paupers that it controls.

Extrapolating the events of the credit crunch and its legacy of unemployment, the £1.5bn regeneration project of Elephant and Castle, and the 2013 Government White Paper that aims to reassess individuals claim on state benefits, Hodgson explores a range of social, economic, historic and political issues. One of the major physical investigations to come out of this line of enquiry was the intensification of the infrastructure within Elephant and Castle. At present, the dense concentration of roads and railway lines in the area is seen as both a physical and social barrier that not only serves its immediate community poorly but additionally discourages investment and development.

Looking at precedents set by past governments in times of recession and, in particular, examples of central investment in mass civic projects for the creation of employment, Hodgson incorporated these findings with the pressing need for increased commuting channels into central London. In a financially crippled economy, new (cost-efficient) elevated roads were imagined relieving congestion, physically separating unrelated commuter traffic from the local community of Elephant and Castle.

Through 3D simulation of this urban strategy, Elephant and Castle's newly envisaged spaces were explored. Speculative renders and collaged imagery of a future cityscape created a tangible vision of infrastructure gradually appropriated and domesticated by the workhouse. Using a re-interpretation of the institutional classical vocabulary (as a familiar dialogue with which to reassure the nervous population), a series of experimental architectural components within the architecture retell the cautionary origins of its creation. These components, often based on originals (such as the triumphal arch), were embellished by paupers and adapted to serve a more contemporary function.

The column classification became intrinsic to reading the building, and the undertones of the paupers adorning the columns became a vehicle for redefining their identity. In the case of the traditional Corinthian column, for example, the piece became adorned with an outstretched pauper that could be read equivocally as ornament, as metaphor or as parable. A worker successfully holding back the tides of recession or a victim crucified and assimilated into the architecture? The process was one of assimilation, reproduction, modification and refabrication in Nylon using Selective Laser Sintering (SLS). For Hodgson: "The final stage of production, the physical print, was essential in making believable the integrity and character of the architectural proposal. The 'Teapot of the Board of Guardians' was a 1:1 fabrication intended to stand alone as a synthesis of the multiple themes of the project. Created for the authorities in charge of the workhouse, its underlying structure represents the architecture and its adornments the cautionary tale, all condensed into a singular object." Imagined as a future relic, a fragment discovered by an archaeologist in years to come, this concluding object tells the story of the workhouse and its legacy.

> Laundry Lady
> Many aspects of the
> workhouse attempts to take
> the extraordinary and make
> it ordinary, in the case of
> the laundry room the aims
> were reverse, it was to take
> the ordinary and make it
> extraordinary. The render
> depicts a insight into the inner
> workings of the workhouse
> with an example of the
> column zoning.

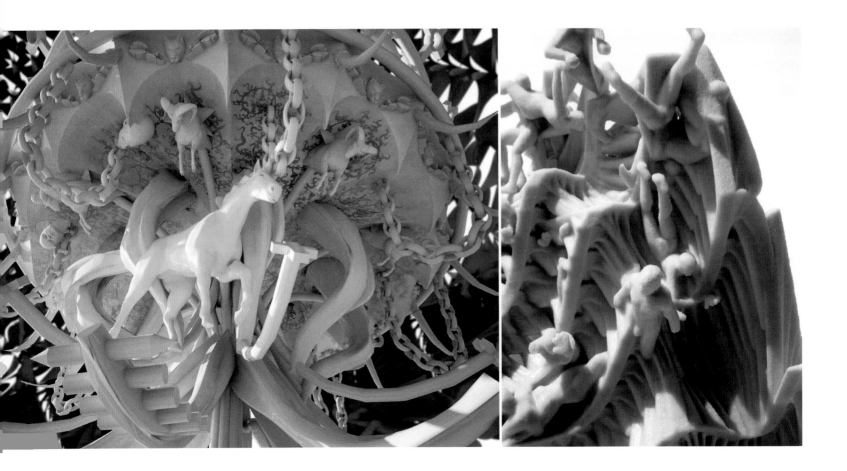

∧ Inhabited travelating chandelier — the object is the physical manifestation of the British coat of arms. It hosts visitors to the workhouse and makes a slow precession through the workhouse building for the visitors to view the spectacle that is the cautionary tale in action.

＞∧ Dome model & render— rapid prototype. The pattern is based upon the classical idea of the repetition of a single form to create a pattern as a decorative feature. In this case, an original shape was extrapolated into a three-dimensional component that in turn was grafted onto a base form using digital scripting. In this way, the architecture was both structure and pattern, turning a visual icon into a building language capable of architectural feats such as the romantic filtration of light.

＞ Column diagram
The illustration is a key into reading the building, utilising the different column types as a method of classifications to zone the different areas. Innit-thian column, Conventus column, Board of Guardians (B.O.G) column, Deus Column, Facultas column.

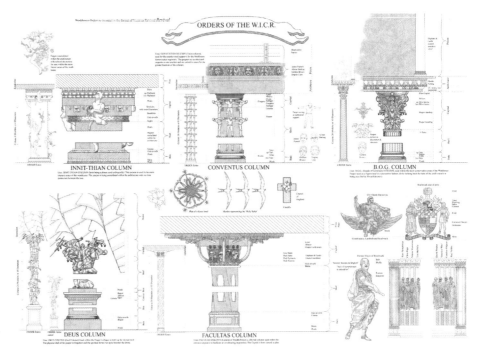

› Teapot—selective laser
sintering (SLS) The 'Teapot
of the Board of Guardians'
was a 1:1 fabrication
intended to stand alone as
a synthesis of the multiple
themes of the project.
Created for the authorities
in charge of the workhouse,
its underlying structure
represents the architecture
and its adornments the
cautionary tale, all condensed
into a singular object. It is
imagined as a future relic,
a fragment discovered by
an archaeologist in years to
come that tells the story of the
workhouse and its legacy.

TAREK SHAMMA

CIRCUS LUMENS

Veneration takes many forms within the church, from individual prayer to pilgrimages that involve the ambulation of ecclesiastical spaces. The animus of a pilgrimage is to reach a state of exaltation, where the sense of the divine becomes palpable. Circus Lumens investigates the design of such a space, engaging visitors' senses through a pilgrimage of texture and light.

Simple Intricacy and The Circle
Manipulating the circle, which defines the elementary geometry of the architecture, an intricate and more elaborate set of relationships is constructed. Through tangency, intersection and orbit, the circle defines the plan, section and every edge condition. The key circle in plan inscribes a cruciform onto which the 14 Stations of the Cross are charted. This defines the pilgrimage route and gives the church specific locations for ceremony.

Pilgrimage of Light
Medieval philosophy, particularly the work of Roger Bacon, discusses a hierarchy of different types of light and sight. They describe direct light as falling on pure souls, refracted light on imperfect souls and reflected light on evil souls. This hierarchy of direct, refracted and reflected is used to define the types of vision: direct vision as that of God, refracted vision as that of angels and reflected vision as that of corporeal beings. The different apparitions of light allow for a range of visual readings of the pilgrimage.

The 14 Stations of the Cross are essential to any church, representing the Via Dolorosa, Christ's passion, charted along the periphery of the space. These begin with the condemnation and sentencing of Christ, to the crucifixion and ultimately his entombment. The visual routes are a series of seven arcs that are defined by connecting three of the 14 stations.

The Story of Material
Shamma interpreted these arcs into three categories: those that deal with the heavenly, corporeal and base stories within the narrative. These arcs define the form of the church: the 'heavenly' define the top, 'corporeal' the middle and 'base' the ground. Similarly, through a physical procession along a materially reflective path, the 'high arcs' define direct light, 'mid arcs' refracted light and the 'base arcs' reflective light. These arcs define the volume of the church as well as the primary structure. The circle is used to define a secondary structure, a mesh compiled of tension cables.

Structure and Texture
The proposed structure is composed of separate shells fitted into the larger frame. Materials explored included marble and onyx, such as alabaster, which would be used as a building block. At large scales, alabaster would still retain translucent qualities that could be accentuated when carved. A church is generally orientated on an east to west axis, therefore examining the site and the sun conditions dictated the way in which the structure needed to be positioned in order that Shamma could explore the way light would infiltrate the building.

Church In The City
In a desire to build to the heavens and contain some sliver of the celestial kingdom under their roof, churches have, for millennia, been forerunners of technological progress in architectural design. They have propelled the way in which materials, such as stone and marble, were used with their tracery and detail, drawing the eye towards the heavens. The site is integral to the design and planned fabrication of Circus Lumens.

Cairo is an old city in the history of the Christian faith and the church sits on the east bank of the River Nile at the heart of the city. The church has absorbed a lot of the Pharaonic rites into its mystery, and the site references that. The building is made entirely of marble quarried from the south. Many monuments built on the banks of the Nile use stone quarried from the south of Egypt and floated up on barges. The relationship between the building and the site is simultaneously very subtle with its references and quite jarring in its physical manifestation.

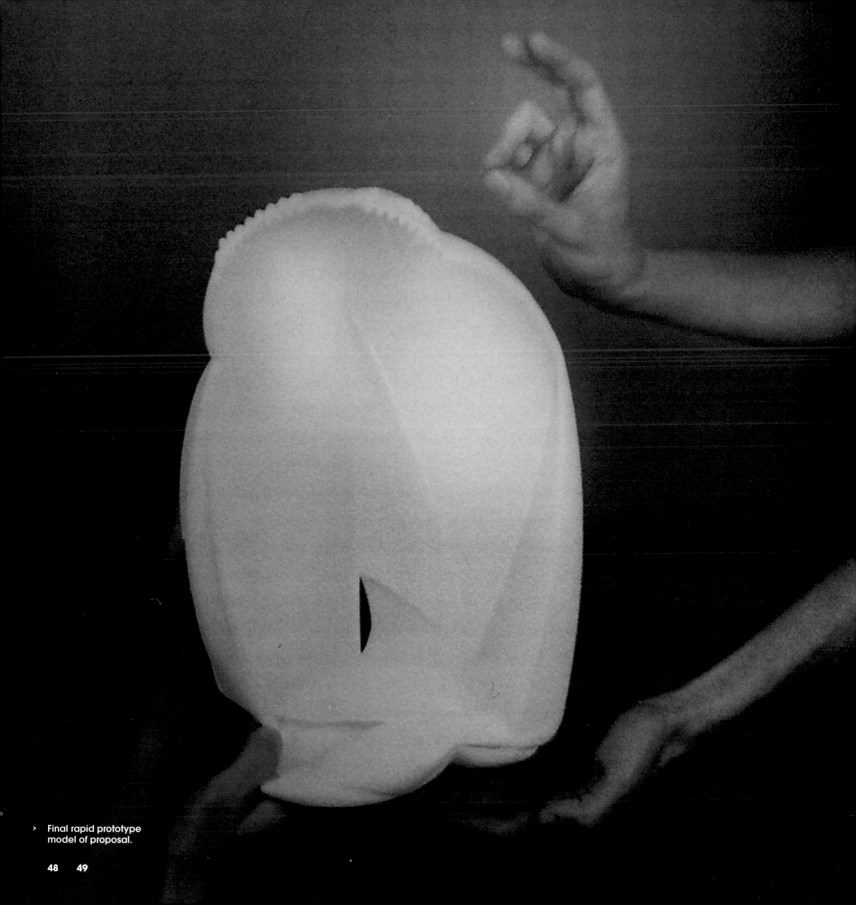

> Final rapid prototype
model of proposal.

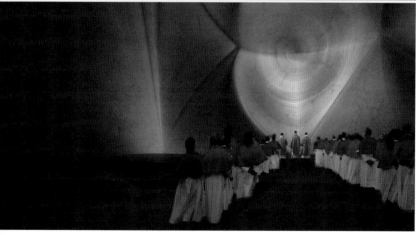

<< Several rapid prototype models
illustrating form and materiality.

< Perspective view of interior.

^ Top view of interior of church.

SCHIZOPHRENIA
& COMPROMISE

BRUCE DAVISON

"The notion of elegance promoted here still gives a certain relevance to Alberti's criterion of beauty: you can neither add, nor subtract without destroying the harmony achieved. Alberti focused on key ordering principles, such as symmetry and proportion. Our current idea of organic integration does not rely on fixed ideal types; neither does it presuppose any proportional system, nor privilege symmetry."[1]

AD Elegance was published in 2007, establishing the term 'elegance' using the work of several key architects and theorists. The only similarity within these works was the rhetorical comparison made to Leon Battista Alberti's 'harmony of the part and whole' project. While they all use some form of digital-assisted means to actuate their argument, the range of tools and techniques is broad, antithetical and, in some cases, fundamentally incompatible. Surprisingly, these disparate design approaches are separately proposed as integral to the achievement of 'elegance.' Ultimately, this results in an opaque and notably inharmonious discourse.

Manuel Delanda and Hani Rashid demonstrate how algorithmic models can balance competing geometries into one 'cohesive' solution. They point to the ability of an algorithm to accurately model the 'metabolic cycles of a simple organism'[2] and presuppose that mathematical elegance, however abstract, is directly translatable to the human experience. By contrast, Preston Scott Cohen argues that locally attenuated geometries, so far incompatible within a globally defined algorithmic model, are essential to achieve 'elegance' at the relativistic scale of human perception.[3] Patrick Schumacher[4] and Mark Foster Gage[5] suggest that the power of the algorithm can be linked to visual criteria, separately proposing parametric models that are coded to allow for localised Gestalt-type configurations in globally cohesive geometries.

Does the dialectical relationship between abstract accuracy and perceptual reality that haunted Alberti and other Renaissance artists (including Leonardo da Vinci) reverberate in the schizophrenic split in the contemporary avant-garde? On one side there are computational design methodologies that promote unheralded complexity and harmony of the part and whole, achieved through high levels of abstraction without concern for attenuation of form in the physical percept. On the other hand, digitally assisted, yet classically informed, modelling techniques are championed as the best means to create forms and voids that can be 'experienced' as harmonious—a protocol that to-date fails to provide a model for complexity and cohesion.

Furthermore, can visual criticality (such as Schumacher and Gage propose) be successfully merged within algorithmic models and, more importantly, what are those visual criteria? This question, in particular, has caused a palpable sense of unease among the digital avant-garde, leading many to wonder if we have missed something. How are we to reconcile this glaring ambiguity in the contemporary notion of 'elegance'?

The power of the algorithm

Let's begin our historical comparison with an overview of the power that algorithms and the abstraction of algebra have brought to contemporary design. These techniques enable, as Greg Lynn has suggested, "multiple affiliations and intricacies".[6] The resulting compositions led Jeff Kipnis to coin the term "intensive coherence".[7] The power of recursion, and the accuracy in algebraically defining relationships, despite their inherently non-visual nature, is intoxicating.

More and more, this trend towards higher levels of abstraction is seen as the most appropriate and complete solution to the architectural design process: "All of your assumptions about how you work are changed because you have to operate at a much higher level of abstraction."[8] Rashid states that: "A new elegance in architecture is ultimately a manifestation of melding cultural significance with the inspired beauty locked within the natural technological and mathematical parameters that have always been architecture's underpinning and scaffold."[9]

Delanda's polemic presupposes an absolute subversion of the embodied percept and suggests that the purity of an abstract mathematical solution guarantees perceived 'elegance'. The emancipation of a disembodied or ecstatic[10] response to geometry is clearly seen in statements such as: "These procedures... should fill us with wonder at what other elegant from-finding processes may be waiting to be discovered."[11] Given this presupposition, it is possible to claim that natural organic processes can be used to develop templates for generative systems and, ultimately, for architectural form.

These protocols, an evolution of complex adaptive system theory,[12] result in mathematical models containing solution sets that are at once metric and non-metric. In simpler terms, these models propose a phase of possible, non-linear, solutions. The abstract implementation of these solution phase sets is staggering. Delanda describes how these manifolds are capable of explaining natural phenomenon that had previously evaded two-dimensional set modelling: "Suddenly, all kinds of periodic behaviour, from convection cells formed by winds or lava flows to the metabolic cycles of simple organisms, became explainable by a single topological feature on an abstract possibility space."[13]

Alberti's secret struggle

While the algorithm is undoubtedly redefining our understanding of linear systems and ordering principles, it would, however, be a mistake to assume that Alberti was convinced of a single metrisable approach. Evidence originally overlooked by leading historian Edwin Panofsky, suggests that in reality he struggled to balance absolute notions of linear measurement with the relativistic nature of human embodied perception; in other words, to balance incompatible metrics.

Jane Andrews Aiken argues that the Renaissance position on a 'rational' method differed considerably from what currently constitutes a broad commitment to Cartesian metrics. She suggests, instead, that the Renaissance trend towards quantification was balanced with a staid commitment to antiquity.[14] It is these competing tendencies that ultimately lead to contradictions in Alberti's text, specifically *De Statua* (1440). While Panofsky credits Alberti with freeing himself from all chains of antiquity, Aiken points to Alberti's differentiation between beauty and accuracy as evidence to the contrary.

Alberti's attempts in *De Statua*, to address this contradiction result in, as Aiken describes, "frequently oblique, if not downright hazy expositions".[15] This lack of clarity has forced many scholars to divorce this writing from texts such as *De Pictura* (*Della pittura* (1436; On Painting). In *De Statua*, Alberti uses mathematics to describe specific practical issues, such as stability. When dealing with the general, however, he argues for a metric reciprocity between order and beauty, in essence proposing that beauty and accuracy are never analogous. To that end, his system of measurement (*exempeda*) was created to maintain a relativistic proportional system, and is inherently concerned with the relative position of the viewer to the object or form and the relative size of these forms in light of the general human dimensions.[16] Aiken also points to Alberti's use of the 'median perpendicular' to attempt to rationalise what Donatello had coined as *contrapposto*, which highlights the value in the position of the viewer.

The glaring inconsistency between the historical struggle and the contemporary algorithmic polemic is that, while it is true that mathematical parameters have, as Rashid states, "always been architecture's scaffolding",[17] these parameters were traditionally filtered through some form of perceptual metric. Harmony or 'elegance' on Delanda's terms presupposes that the direct human interpretation of space is directly correlated to the purity of an abstract algebraic solution set, overlooking the necessary translation or encoding.

Metrical reciprocity

Cohen argues that a re-invention of projective geometry is the means to employ a perceptual metric in the design process and considers this the only approach to achieve 'elegance' at the scale of the human experience. His rhetoric calls for an expert manual manipulation of a digital model and he consistently addresses the interiority of the architectural project. In his opinion, projected geometries with their base in relativistic proportion are "most susceptible with an engagement of production and reception of architecture". [18]

Cohen presents the Tel Aviv Museum of Art project to elucidate his argument and points to some areas in the design where projective geometry is used to create astonishing moments of non-linear proportion and attenuation. Despite his masterful use of projective geometry, and while specific rules for algebraic recursion could be possible, systemisation seems unattainable. Thus, achieving complex inter-articulation and inter-dependencies at larger scales using algorithmic protocol is unlikely. While his work resolves (as he states) Alberti's difficulty in producing a "metrical reciprocity", [19] it does so only in very specific instances and falls short of providing a model for cohesive complexity.

Two dimensional vision theory in n-dimensional space

The importance of encoding visual latency, simultaneously at local and global levels, within a complex algebraically defined model, is recognised by Gage and Schumacher, who suggest that the solution to the contemporary dilemma can be found in Gestalt theory. Gage states emphatically that, "elegance creates a topology from which a figure can be read, calibrated through isolated views and expertly calibrated moments". [20] Schumacher agrees that the form in relation to void clarity must be definable on embodied terms, stating explicitly that the ability to interpret organisation and iconicity should be the primary goal of 'elegance'. [21]

In order to address this concern for vision, Schumacher suggests the coding of the Gestalt laws into algorithmic protocols. [22] Schumacher has stated his interest in algebraically linking Gestalt, as a dynamic constraint into emergent and generative models, such as those described by Delanda and Rashid.

This, however, presents a sizeable challenge as the Gestalt phenomenon, such as proximity, similarity, continuation and closure, is well documented in two-dimensional testing and analysis. However, the 'scaffolding' required for three- or four-dimensional implementation has so far proved elusive. Experimental psychologists have for sometime questioned the appropriateness of two-dimensionality, abstraction and archetype in the evaluation of the three-dimensional human perceptual experience.

"Most psychologists rely upon the use of two-dimensional diagrams in their perceptual experiments. If one assumes this separation of picture and world perception, then such diagrams reveal little (if not nothing) about world perception." [23]

da Vinci's unfinished business

The difficulty in translating the three-dimensional experience into two dimensions was a primary concern to the Renaissance artists. Hidden in da Vinci's unpublished works are observations that help to construct a better picture of the Renaissance struggle to create an absolute classification of perspective using a linear method. da Vinci and his fellow artists were not easily able to relinquish their conviction in relativistic proportions and forms

of curvilinear perspective. This conviction was grounded in the design methodology that had been in existence since antiquity. [24] Aiken suggests that Alberti's contemporaries, led by da Vinci, considered his treaty on perspective to be fundamentally flawed with regards to optics. [25]

In da Vinci's unpublished work on optics, we find what may be significant lessons for today's *avant garde*, wishing to code a perceptual metric. da Vinci criticised Alberti's treatise on perspective as gross generalisation, and acknowledges that the simple perspective was no more than, "a workshop device, and natural vision as operating quite differently, with light impulses being registered in the eye not at a point, as required by the simple method, but all over the surface of the eye". [26] Although he was never able to propose an explanation for its true natural process, his notes outlined the approximations that completely failed to address "the moving eye" and "distortions occurring from close viewpoints".

More than 60 years ago, John White [27] described how da Vinci was well aware of the importance of curvilinear perspective, not simply as an artistic method, but more importantly as a model for the functioning of the embodied perceptual mechanism. Kim Veltman demonstrated how renaissance painters used alternative non-empirical models, not just for illusory affect but as a stringent model for a vision that have been overlooked by Panofsky and other cultural historians. [28] Veltman insists that a closer assessment of these techniques, not simply as illusionary tools but as alternative models for human vision, will shed new light on the importance of non-empirical modes of Renaissance composition.

A new vision for vision

The preceding analysis of the Renaissance struggle for classification of order and beauty has revealed that the greatest point of contention at the time, apparent in Alberti's own texts and among the sentiments of his contemporaries, was with regards to the geometric construct of vision. While most 20th century artists, architects and theorists, under the influence of paradigmatic movements in philosophy and art, had little interest in developing new research on the topic, there were some who questioned the *status quo*.

Rudolf Arnheim, whose text Visual Thinking [29] was instrumental in disseminating the cubist mantra into architectural discourse, originally believed that the cubist movement had successfully materialised the tenets of special relativity. However, after Arnheim approached Einstein with his conviction, Einstein responded with a poignant criticism of the analogy, stating that: "A multiplicity of systems of coordinates is not needed for its (special relativity) representation. It is completely sufficient to describe the whole mathematically in relation to one system of coordinates." [30] After which Arnheim became intrigued by the notion of hyperbolic perspective and Riemannian geometry, leading one to safely assume that Arnheim's interest in space-time did not fade, it simply evolved.

In his review of Robert Hansen's proposal for the 'artistic' use of curvilinear space in his essay 'Hansen and curvilinear perspective' [31], Arnheim accuses Hansen of not recognising the potential of this technique beyond mere 'artistic expression'. He writes: "Depth (in Cubist work) was restricted to orthogonal recession because lateral recession would have to go beyond the deformation of angles; it calls for the deformation of straight shapes." [32] Arnheim criticises Hansen, not for employing illusion, but for failing to realise how this hyperbolic construct could legitimise a new paradigm for critical direction for art. Arnheim's revelation adheres to a non-linear structure for evaluating cognitive process of visual perception.

It was not simply art and architectural theory that was held in limbo on the issue of vision—cognitive science was also embroiled in a battle between information theory in computer science and functionalism in philosophy. [33] More recently, scientists are taking a new interest in the careful geometric analysis of the direct functioning of vision. Experimental psychologist Robert French concedes that while a data set replicating all the factors that influence vision cannot be "rigorously deduced", he insists that a rich discourse can be found in the direct geometry of embodied vision.[34]

Researchers have begun to test new modelling software and computational techniques that could provide methodologies to analyse true three- and four-dimensional vision theory. Antonio Battro has provided a convincing description of how this three-dimensional framework might function and suggests that vision works on a metric that closely mimics Riemannian geometry.[35]

Therefore, does the same technology that has caused the contemporary schism in architectural theory offer a solution for our final emancipation as digitally assisted designers? Could computation help to reopen the work that eluded da Vinci and, in doing so, develop a platform for metrical reciprocity between algebraic prowess and visual criticality. Or are algorithmic techniques fundamentally at odds with what Cohen considers to be sacred to design and the ultimate reception of architecture?

What is definite is that if we assume that computational design presupposes the complete critical reception of architecture, we could be setting ourselves up to repeat the generalisations of Alberti, which relegated attenuation and non-linear proportion to centuries of neglect only to be rediscovered in the Baroque. We should take the lead offered by cognitive science and embrace a new vision for vision—a three- and four-dimensional framework for vision that will allow us to navigate as empowered architects, designing critically receptive architecture, in the brave new world of computationally assisted design.

1   Arguing for Elegance — P Schumacher, *Architectural Design: Elegance* (2007).
2   Material Elegance — M Delanda, *Architectural Design: Elegance* (2007).
3   Elegance, Attenuation, Geometry — P S Cohen, *Architectural Design: Elegance* (2007).
4   See 1 above.
5   Deus Ex Machina — M F Gage, *Architectural Design: Elegance* (2007).
6   *Folding in architecture*, G Lynn (2004).
7   Critical discriminations (lecture) — J Kipnis and Syracuse University School of Architecture (2006).
8   Lars Hesselgren, Director at KPF London — stated in Bentley's Generative Components Promotional Video.
9   Performing Elegance — H Rashid, *Architectural Design: Elegance* (2007).
10 The Dislocation of the Architectural Self — D Goldblatt, *Journal of Aesthetics and Art Criticism*
11 See 2 above.
12 *Collected works* — K Gödel and S Feferman (1986).
13 See 2 above.
14 Leon Battista Alberti's System of Human Proportions — J A Aiken, *Journal of the Warburg and Courtauld Institutes* (1980).
15 Ibid.
16 Ibid.
17 See 9 above.
18 See 3 above.
19 Ibid.
20 See 5 above.
21 See 1 above.
22 Simultaneity & Latency, Perception, Insight, Orientation — Zaha Hadid Meisterklasse, University of Applied Arts Vienna (2007), Studio brief.
23 *The Ecological Approach to Visual Perception* — J J Gibson (1979).
24 Systematic Deviations from Ordinary Rectilinear Construction — W Johnson, *International Journal of Mechanical Science* (1997).
25 See 14 above.
26 Leonardo's Eye — J S Ackerman, *Journal of the Warburg and Courtauld Institutes* (1978).
27 Developments in Renaissance Perspective (I) — John White, *Journal of the Warburg and Courtauld Institutes* 12 (1/2) (1949)
28 Perspective, Anamorphosis and Vision — K H Veltman (1986) *Marburger Jahrbuch*, Marburg, Vol 21.
29 *Visual Thinking* — R Arnheim (1969).
30 Cubism and Relativity with a Letter of Albert Einstein — P M Laporte, *Leonardo* (1988).
31 This Curving World: Hyperbolic Linear Perspective — R Hansen, *Journal of Aesthetics and Art Criticism* (1973).
32 See 29 above.
33 *The Body in Pain: The Making and Unmaking of the World* — E Scarry (1985).
34 The Geometry of Visual Space — R French, *Noûs*, Vol 21, No 2 (1987).
35 Visual Riemannian space versus cognitive Euclidean space — A M Battro, *Synthese*

YUTING JIANG

SHADOW PLAY

The project considers projected shadows as an extremely sophisticated phenomenon. An experimental piece of work on how to utilise projected and enclosed space, the project proposes scenarios that allow architecture to 'change' form and function and be responsive to its environment, specifically in relation to light and shadow. It proposes a constructed domain that continuously opposes and evolves between light and shadow, revealing and concealing its architecture. Its theme oscillates between the immaterial and the physical, the intangible and the measurable.

Process of Shadow Space
Exploring the spatial definition of a shadow space, a shadowgraph prototype is created—a three-dimensional construction of a series of two-dimensional shadow silhouettes, forming a volume of space to be deconstructed and inhibited. The same projected shadows set out the boundaries of the constructed realm as the animated projection is viewed on a screen without preserving physical puppets. The volumetric model, representing the shadow space, consists of two puppets in fighting scenarios. By self-orbiting to a particular angle, the silhouette of the figure appears through the projection. As one preserves it at a certain angle, elements become visible, while others vanish through the movement of the shadowgraph volumetric model—essential for the meaning of the image to appear.

The hybrid-puppet is the intersection of the two projection volumes—the light beams become tangible solids as two beams are projected onto the object from separated angles and the object is revealed by its two different shadows. The second shadowgraph volumetric model consists of different figures. As the light beam shoots through the solidified volume, the model itself is a representation of the hybrid shadow, through which figures are revealed by projecting light from appropriate angles.

Based on the same methodology of the hybrid-shadowgraph construction, the next model's emphasis is more on the formation of the shadow volume and the destruction of the volume into tectonically / architecturally defined lattices, facets and volume. Studies of the relationship between positive and negative space imply function into the formatted form itself, setting out the baseline for this final year project.

These prototype studies led to the final proposal for an experimental movie screen and a projection canopy in Campo de Fiori, Rome. The building addresses the interplay and experimentation between immateriality and ornamentation, forms and function, and immateriality and the physical. The proposal asks for realisations and representations of the intangible phenomenal through which spatial qualities could be quested and created as playful and self-involving scenarios.

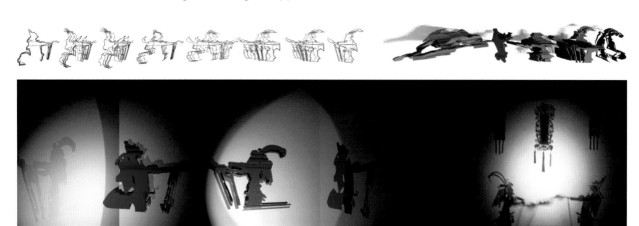

< Shadowgraph volumetric
model illustrates the morphosis
of two puppet figures within
a fighting scenario.

> Perspective view of the
experimental movie screen
and projection canopy in
Campo de Fiori set in the
heart of Rome.

'HEAR HERE'—AN ACOUSTIC THEATRE MODULATED BY ITS OCCUPANTS

The project concerns itself with sound and the body aiming to generate a physical construct that, while taking physics, music and architecture into account, sets out to explore how space can be understood through sound.

Sound is an integral part of the way we understand the space surrounding us. Size, quality, timbre, texture and the atmosphere of a space can all be inferred by the way in which we experience sound. Based on ideas from the Suffolk island of Orford Ness, the project developed a preoccupation with the acoustic qualities of circular spaces and ambient sonic landscapes.

If architecture is the manipulation of space, then the built form is a way of capturing the ambient. At the core of this question is the way space is experienced as a function of the sounds found both within and around the space, and the sounds that result from occupancy of the space.

The building is the final movement in the score of this experiential journey concerning itself with sound and the body. By giving concepts physical form, the experience can be explored. It is a tourable, demountable structure. By exploring concepts of resonance, reflection, absorption, forced and natural, the work creates a 'sonic geography' framed within a physical construct that invites you to explore, listen, improvise and experience.

Comprising a monocoque, aluminium, open cone wrapped within a closed, tensioned, plywood structure, the two spaces act in combination to echo the form of the ear. The outer ear is the space in-between the wooden and aluminium skin, and it has a soft acoustic. Sounds reflect around the walls in a whispering gallery-type nature. The audience follow the sounds around the dark outer corridor and are 'cleansed' of what John Cage would describe as the "chaos of the everyday sounds". The journey around the structure leads the audience into the inner drum. The aluminium cone is open to the world. It is bright and metallic, both in form and acoustic.

This project combines the world of manufacture, with the ephemeral nature of the ambient. The structure becomes a frame for the sound to exist. The audience are invited to enter and listen. The inner metal skin acts as an instrument, listening to the outer world and playing it back through a set of speakers. These sounds reflect and reverberate around the space.

The sound pavilion exists, it is here to be experienced, for the user to enter and listen within. Essentially the pavilion is an ear capturing sounds from its immediate environment. Its geometries can intensify, resonate and distort these found sounds and act as a passive instrument, playing sounds of the city based on the occupier's position within the structure.

PANELS WATERJET CUT FROM 1500 x 3000 x 2mm ALUMINIUM SHEETS

WOODEN PARTS CNC ROUTED FROM 1220 x 2440 x 18mm PLYWOOD

WOODEN SKIN HAND CUT FROM 1500 x 500 x 3mm PLYWOOD

‹ Exploding view of
building parts.

› Kit of parts.

< Making the building.

^ Final proposal on site.

Founded and directed by Julien de Smedt (also co-founder of PLOT), JDS Architects currently employs some 50 people with offices in Copenhagen, Brussels and Oslo. JDS Architects is a multi-disciplinary office focusing on architecture and design, from large scale planning to furniture. Rich with multiple expertises, our office is fuelled by talented designers and experienced architects that jointly develop projects from early sketches to on-site supervision.

All of which, regardless of scale, outlines an approach that is affirmatively social in its outcome, enthusiastic in its ambition and professional in its process. At the core of our architecture is the ability to take a fresh look at design problems through experienced eyes. Our approach aims at turning intense research and analysis of practical and theoretical issues into the driving forces of our design.

By continuously developing rigorous methods of analysis and execution, JDS Architects is able to combine innovative thinking and efficient production.

JDS Architects has completed a number of early competitions, many of which have now been realised, demonstrating our ability to think about architecture in new innovative ways without sacrificing practicality or buildability. JDS Architects has also obtained numerous honours and awards for our work in Europe and abroad. We have received three Mies van der Rohe award nominations for our VM House, Mountain, and Maritime Youth House

projects, as well as a Golden Lion at 2004 Venice Biennale for our Stavanger Concert Hall project. Other major awards include a World Architecture Festival award for Best Housing project, an AR+D award, and the Forum Prize for best project in Scandinavia. Most recently, Julien De Smedt was awarded the Netherlands highest architectural honour, the Rotterdam Maaskant Prize.

INTERVIEW O2

JDS
ARCHITECTS

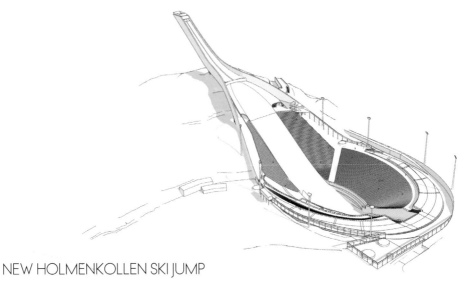

NEW HOLMENKOLLEN SKI JUMP

Holmenkollen hill plays a significant part in identifying Oslo, with its characteristic profile a clear icon in Oslo's panorama. It's a building beyond conventions and one of Oslo's most visited tourist attractions.

Conceptually, the project works with three stages of visibility: The far-away panorama, the zoom-in at the foot of the slope and the view from the top.

To emphasise the silhouette, the shape is sharp and simply cut, using the given wind protection profile and offsetting it parallel down, creating a smooth-bended rectangle hosting the slope, the main elevators and the top in-run program. The top is cut horizontally to accommodate a viewing platform and the Knoll building is moved further up the hill, serving as anchor point for the structure, letting it cantilever and avoid a disruptive structural support. From a distance, the structure will appear as a milky-white sharp profile extended by a light beam diffusing into the sky.

Relocating the knoll establishes it as the direct access point to the top in-run and creates a prime location for the restaurant. The new knoll forms part of the landscape, somewhat similar to the exiting ski museum. It also creates a grand viaduct for the existing road and an accessible and centrally located drop-off and main entrance. An elevator will run straight to the top of the in-run.

Diagrammatically, the top in-run is four levels of different program, but with the elevator penetrating through and various other openings, it becomes an open coherent space mixing the different usages together, with the open-air platform ending the visit with spectacular views.

The facade is perceived as one continuous band, setting off at the top of the slope, running alongside the landing hill and the spectator stands encapsulating the whole arena in a white framing glow. It will be lit up from within, between structure and glass to implement a diffused misty image. From afar, the colour will melt into one image depending on the seasons or time of day, but up close a gradient of transparent, translucent and opaque zones will reveal the different depths of the program and construction.

Interview with Julien de Smedt

Q. To many young architects hoping to start their own firm, JDS's success is inspirational. On what principles was the office founded?

Work hard, party hard...

Q. How do you link different modes of computation from schematic design research to construction and at what stage do computers enter your design process?

We're sort of low tech. Computers are omnipresent, but we're not placing them above other means of creation. Our most important computer tool is the Internet, our most important creative tool is discussion, and to formulate ideas into shapes we mostly work with physical models. The common idea that computers are more powerful because they're more advanced is false—there's nothing more interactive than a physical model. In the investigation process what matters is speed, speed of ideas translated with immediacy. This is only possible with models as we're immediately able to see them and manipulate them live. This is also possible with computers, but there's a difference in speed and a distance in physicality.

Q. JDS works on projects of various scales—how does the role of the digital change to account for these varied interventions?

In some cases, projects are too big (almost territorial) to be investigated in model form. The process of mapping is easier with a computer. Paradoxically, the bigger and much smaller scales are better handled with computers. If we design a lamp, for instance, it is the way the light comes out that matters and that's very demanding to do as a prototype in physical form—it's much easier to do with renderings.

Q. On multiple occasions you have stated your interest in social issues and social interactions. How do these translate into your design aesthetic and how do your modes of working facilitate these interests?

We don't have aesthetic concerns—we're interested in effects. The projects we do are aimed at enhancing social and urban interactions. We manipulate volumes to amplify potentials and reconnect urban conditions.

Q. As an architect and a teacher (Rice University and the University of Kentucky), how do you use the digital in teaching, research and practice?

It's not dissimilar to the way we work at the office. I motivate my students to research and overproduce to create sufficient knowledge and information to start a discussion. In order to make our work relevant in the academic circle, we consider it to be real; not in the way that we limit ourselves to regulations, codes and political constraints, but rather in the mindset of working towards a goal that will have concrete consequences.

I only teach in the US (so far) so I always work via emails. It's very interesting to insist on the fact that every idea we have should be communicated by simple means, such as emails. It will make my students learn how to focus on the right elements and know their priorities.

Q. How do you place your work in the context of other architects, and what work by other young artists / designers / architects do you find interesting?

We live in a world of overproduction and individual proclaim. Everyone can do anything and promote it. Sites like Dezeen, for example, constantly publish single designs by straight-out-of, or still-in-school, designers. The world today is all about design. There are an exponential number of new design magazines, design awards, design conferences, design shows—we're design saturated. Therefore, I think it's completely irrelevant to call out a few names or designs that I'm interested in.

Q. What advice would you offer graduates today who are coming out of education?

To apply to my office—we're interested in intelligence.

Q. Where do you see your own practice in the next five years?

I make my own plans and navigate towards them, but do not need to predict the future. I'm very flexible and interested in new opportunities, so these plans also tend to evolve, be combined to new plans and mutate. I don't promise something that I know I will myself have manipulated in the course of its making.

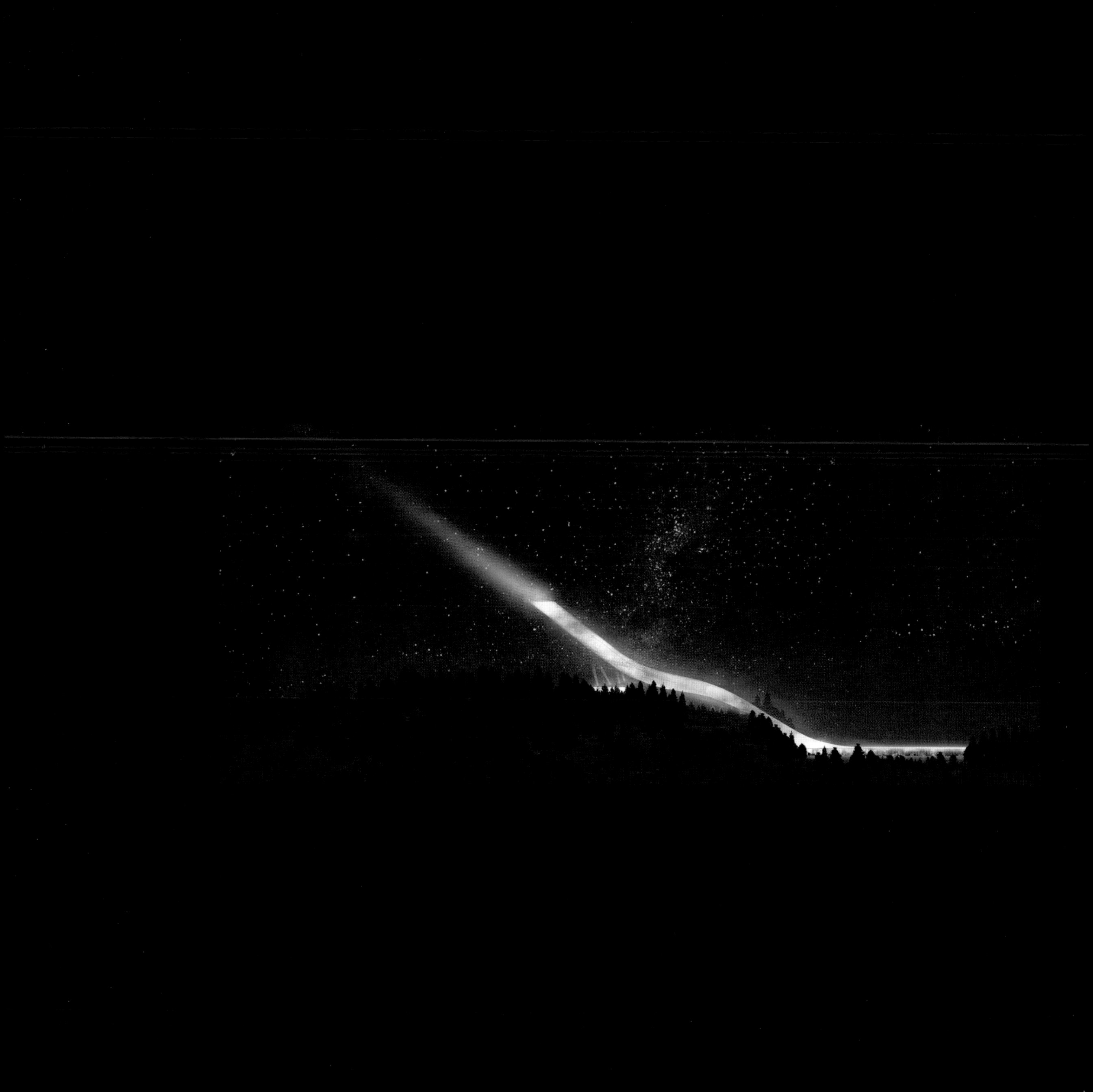

CHRISTIAN KERRIGAN

THE 200 YEAR CONTINUUM

This article explains the construction of the fictional project of growing a ship in the Kingley Vale, West Sussex—one of the last remaining Yew forests. The narrative tells the story of the Amber Clock. Defined as a symbiotic fictive performance, a ship is grown over 200 years, displaying the choreography between a natural system of growth and the artificial presence of man-made interventions. The narrative describes how the trees are shaped, using elaborate Bonsai techniques, to form the ship's structure. As the trees grow, the ship emerges in the forest; its shape inside the forest also alters the sound of the trees, making the ship an acoustic instrument within its augmented eco-system. Meanwhile, as artificial and wild systems are choreographed, the natural production of resin is harvested from the Yew trees as a method for measuring time. In creating this fictional narrative, I explore the possibilities of time in relationship to technology and the natural world.

The Process

In my practice, I create documentation that 'records forward' a dialogue about our society and its ongoing relationship with technology and the natural world. 'Recording forward' is a methodology I have developed in order to raise propositions about our current age. The documentation takes the form of texts, drawings and installations, made and experienced between a digital media and real world viewing. My notebook, which I carry with me, forms the first space in which each mythology is recorded.

I start by writing sentences referring to each 'middle story', which in their initial ambiguity generate the basis from which I mould my narrative. The reflexive dialogue between visual material, historical reference and writing continues throughout my working process until a moulded final piece has been reached, taking the form of predominantly digital mediums of expression.

The Beginning Of Middle Story: The Amber Clock

This work began as a series of drawings exploring the worlds of artificial and natural systems, and developed the forest's choreography as a metaphor for our relationship to the natural world. I chose Kingley Vale as a theoretical site for my intervention as it contained existing historical narratives and mythologies that form the background on which to construct my own narrative. I formulated my theoretical framework based on existing and imagined mythologies regarding man's relationship to nature, so as to speak of society's shifting focus and interpretation of its surrounding environment. From the assumption that nature remains, itself, a very slow changing system, the narrative explains how natural and artificial systems could potentially work symbiotically to generate a new kind of dynamic architectural phenomenon, whose effect would be best observed over an extended period of time.

My production process involved successive drawing studies choreographing the narrative and generating direction for the complete body of work. Joseph Beuys described the focus on drawing and image as a convergence of thought and space on which to create a dialogue. My drawing process involved mapping various spaces within the forest using 3D modelling, the making of which organised the spatial and visual language for the space-time continuum and provided a visual 'test space' for the narrative to exist and play out *in situ*. As the narrative depicts a time-based continuum, drawing assumes the role of recording the process in a forward-looking scenario. The narrative has the ability to create a journey through new territories, navigating time and space by defining a path by which the audience may experience the world one has created.

I also incorporated elements from the art of Bonsai and the input of relevant real world scenarios offered by Martin Bridge, dendrochronologist at the Institute of Archaeology, University College London. He described the body language of trees and pre-empted how the natural system will cope within my narrative. As the narrative is set over 200 years, it is the use of drawing within the virtual landscape that provides the facility to stretch investigations beyond real world experiments and logic. To reference Joseph Beuys, from a passage on the artist by his chief photographer, Caroline Tisdall: "The widening of language is the key to the process of change in thinking. For Beuys the widening of language came through drawing. Drawing becomes a way to reach areas that are limited by speech or abstract thinking alone, to suspend all notions of limits or limitations of a field so that it encompasses everything. The widening principle means the pulling together of man's experience through time."[1]

> Macresco, 2006
Digital drawing. Description: The
mechanisms shown describe
how the tree grows into the
formwork to take the shape of
the bow of the ship. The natural
system can be artificially trained
over time.

The Narrative

The narrative defines a spatial and time-based metaphor of future scenarios in which our society may find itself. With advancing technology, new mythologies will emerge and our society will inhabit newly-imagined worlds only navigated through man's extension by technological means. The narrative begins citing where society currently stands in the history of the dialogue between technology and the natural world, followed by presenting the existing historical mythologies surrounding Kingley Vale.

Hidden Architectures Find Niches As Moist Technology

In our evolution, we are now capable of creating design criteria to manipulate natural growth and development. Through stem-cell research and making at the nano-scale, the spectrum of opportunity now open to the exploration of complex systems has revolutionised our existing understanding of the natural world and our relationship to mortality.

Walk Down The Chalk Road Past The Meadows

On the chalk downland of northwest Chichester is Kingley Vale, covering roughly 300 acres in a combe, the oldest trees stand at around 900 years, while must of the rest of the landscape is approximately 500 years old.

The mythology behind the planting of the forest tells of a marauding Viking war band that came to attack Chichester in the 9th century. The trees descend from those planted as a memorial on the battlefield site.

In adding my narrative to this mythology, I introduce three key players—nature, technology and time: 'nature' being the natural system of growth for the newly planted Yew trees, the planting, insertion and evolution of this site choreograph nature and its hidden architectures; 'technology' as an artificial system that is created to fulfil a given task, generating the narrative for the system to alter and steer nature into producing a hidden vessel; and, the engagement of 'time' makes the forest a unique site for new spatial fields, the slow maturing of distance and time evokes a powerful sense of technology as longevity.

No-One Is Ever Seen Entering Or Leaving

Across the lake, the ship's silhouette evolves as a hidden piece of mythical architecture; its form is controlled by individual corsets wrapped around a tree trunk, manipulating the growth of separate parts of the vessel. As the tree grows through the corset, the shape of the designed armature controls the extrusion. The Macresco harvests the growth imperative of trees; it is structuring the launching pier, hull and rudder as the wet system grows dense. As the ship ages, hybrid systems interact with the object. The cell structure at the nano-scale alters, while natural ecosystems find new relationships with the growing object. Climatic changes, both globally and in the microcosm, act as an added force in defining the ship's evolution, since the forest itself weathers and ages.

In the Amber Clock, a corset wrapped around the tree trunk is used to bleed resin to generate the clock's momentum. It acts as the calibrating device between the

∧ The Amber Clock, 2006
Digital drawing. Description: An 'Amber clock' is strapped to the tree trunk to keep track of passing time. The resin from the tree bleeds into the 200 year hour glass, much like Egyptian water clocks, it slowly fills and when it is full, the clock stops, signaling the end of the system.

< ^ Obelisk Map, 2007
Digital drawing. Description:
The ship's figurehead is a
carved ornamental and
painted figure erected on
the bow of ships, as an iconic
symbol of its time. In this project
the figurehead evolves from
the splitting of the Yew
tree as an iconographic
piece between nature
and technology.

< Ships Obelisk, 2007
Digital drawing. Description:
Spliced apparatus from the
tree is grown towards the final
stages of the ship. As it leaves
the forest, its journey to find,
locate and exhume the obelisk
from the granite landscape
is achieved.

< ∨ The 200 Year Elevation
2007, Digital drawing.
Description: As the ship
arrives in its location, it is
then disassembled, to cut
slots and markers extracting
the stone from the ground.
The sheathing of the obelisk
in transportation forms the
hull of the ship as it relocates.

> The Continuum Technologies,
2006, Digital drawing.
Description: The technologies
offered in the narrative exploring
the possibilities of time in
relationship to technology
and the natural world.

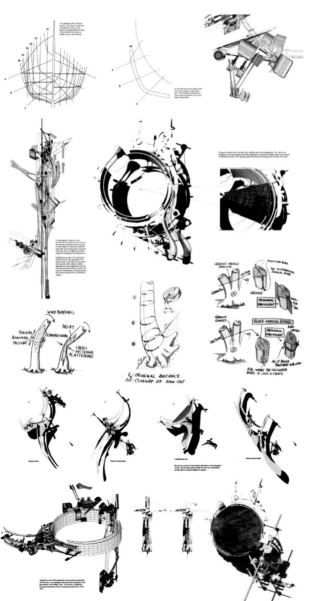

trees' timescale and the artificial system and as an artefact for a generation 200 years from now to find, reconstruct and add to the system's history. The clocking can register the age of the system, and tweak the degree of tension according to the maturing of the forest. As the hourglass fills over time, the resin slowly hardens and the clock begins to jam. Ultimately, the volume of the hourglass is filled, the clock stops and the system is complete.

By manipulating the density of the trunks, the alteration of the forest begins to take on the acoustic resonance of a ship, and the system produces an instrument, each tree an individually tuned, natural instrument.

The Conclusion
Narrative complete, I posted online 3D drawings from the project and a short blurb defining the objective. I received a response from a father and his young son who had gone to visit Kingley Vale in search of my growing ship. "We spent hours," he wrote, "roaming the forest looking for this... any clues?"

The Amber Clock began as a project seeking to describe a complex system using detailed drawings and text. The striking and unanticipated conclusion to the creation of the project is in the reaction of this man and his son. By offering the narrative to a public forum, blurring the boundaries between reality and fiction, it turned an architectural vision into a myth. Each time I speak of the Amber Clock, I am perpetuating the myth and my primary objective can be realised—to speak of the idea of environmental and manmade interactions as a means of communicating a new disposition to future natures or synthetic ecologies. This conclusion, in the aftermath of the Amber Clock, led to the inception of The 200 Year Continuum.

1   Joseph Beuys: *We Go This Way*—C Tisdall (1998)

CHARLOTTE THOMAS

VASCULAR ATTRACTION MEDIATOR

The scheme is a series of art gallery pavilions and horse stables, investigating algorithmic design of circulation and environmental mediation informed by Niemeyer's undulating volumes within the Park Ibirapuera, São Paulo.

An arrangement of cone-shaped spaces become inhabitable light wells and ventilation pipes, providing a mixed-use public building. Synchronising the movement of both environmental and cultural flows, Thomas investigated algorithmic organisational systems to manage and choreograph circulation routes. In critique of the existing large-scale monolithic expo-halls within the park, she proposes smaller scale 'bundles' of vertical channels aligned to the 'attraction agents' of prevailing sun, wind and circulation flows. These inhabitable channels serve as ventilation, light diffusion chimneys and spiralling-ramped galleries, creating a dialogue between the art collection and the external environment.

Essential to the environmental design of the proposal, Thomas algorithmically optimises natural ventilation for the equestrian facilities and the diffusion of light to limit sun damage to the art collection. Synchronising the movement of both environmental and cultural flows, Thomas investigated organisational systems to manage and choreograph flows at three different scales: master plan, building (global) and component (micro).

Rather than the top-down, homogeneous organisations of the orthogonal grid (or the highly deterministic Lindenmayer-system (L-system) configuration), the West, Brown and Enquist (WBE) metabolic theory of ecology was employed to sculpt and script the architecture. The WBE theory is based upon vascular movement within plants and lungs, characterised as a space-filling network that branches hierarchically to supply all parts of a three-dimensional body. Each biofication of this branched network is a power of itself to three-quarters. Distributing the pavilions across the park, Thomas employed what she terms as 'multiple scale attraction field scripting'. Again using the WBE logic, a field organisation was algorithmically formed creating gradations of connectivity between existing and emergent new architecture.

Thomas's interest in the digital translation of mathematics into architecture can be seen by her aim to realise the spatial potential within the Enneper minimal surface curve. At a building scale, Thomas rearticulated the interior of this monolithic minimal surface structure, tailoring pavilions across the site to respond to specific environmental forces at varying times of the day or year. She utilised an attractor script to map the lines of the sun path and wind rose onto the Enneper shell, producing a new curve and tapering apertures according to the sun or prevailing winds.

In other zones, she proliferated light-diffusing components along this new curve by undertaking computational tests of the Enneper surface as a possible shading device. Thomas's proposal with its highly ornamental, environmental and pedestrian movement flows, sets up an architecture of motion and dialogue, challenging the 20th century modernist notion that the museum should be a neutral 'white box', stationary, quietly serving the art work it holds.

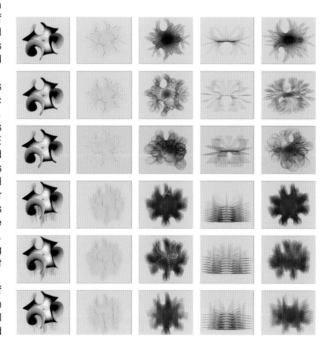

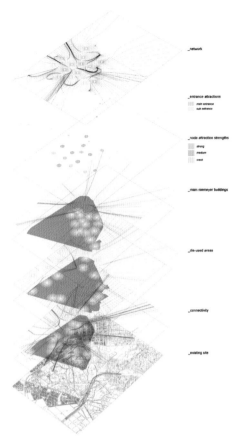

_network

_entrance attractions
    main entrance
    sub entrance

_node attraction strengths
    strong
    medium
    weak

_main niemeyer buildings

_dis-used areas

_connectivity

_existing site

< To articulate the open space of the shell of the enneper minimal surface Thomas devised a system defined by points and objects, utilising the inherent algorithm of the enneper's pointgrid in combination with nodes of attraction therefore informing the surface by external environment.

> By varying the attraction / repellence Thomas was able to categorise different nodes in terms of different categories of activities. The diverse levels of attraction add specificity to the nodes giving them a hierarchy. She classified the entrances into two categories main (blue) and sub (green) as well as grading the node positions of the pavilions on the site into three magnetic strengths; high (red), medium(grey and low (magenta). The idea is that the red pavilions will be the most frequently visited and the flows will be the most intense from the blue starting points.

marcosandmarjan is a London-based studio founded by Marcos Cruz and Marjan Colletti in 2000, which combines the practice and teaching of architecture, along with experimental design research. The work has been extensively published and exhibited, including: the Actions re Form exhibitions in Coimbra and Munich in 2002; the São Paulo Biennial in 2003; participation in the Metaflux exhibition at the Venice Biennale in 2004; and, the solo exhibition Interfaces / Intrafaces at the iCP Hamburg and TU Braunschweig in 2005/06. Apart from numerous exhibition installations, they built two pavilions and the general layout for the 75th Lisbon Book Fair in Portugal, and worked on a large entertainment complex in Beijing, which they won as part of an invited competition in 2004. Recently, their project was a runner-up for the invited competition of a sales centre in Cairo.

PROJECT FOR THE 75TH LISBON BOOK FAIR

The project proposal is characterised by a variety of spaces and atmospheres to be discovered while walking along the Boulevards on both sides of the Parque Eduardo VII. Against the traditional layout of stands and pavilions which were historically aligned in parallel rows, this proposal positions the stands surrounding several open areas in order to form small squares with a strong urban feeling. These spaces are differentiated by arrangement and colour, acting simultaneously as resting spaces and areas where specific activities for the publishers can take place.

The access to the fair is permitted from different sides and punctuated by main public pavilions. But it is on the north side that the most iconographic infrastructures are implanted: the information pavilion on the top of the eastern boulevard, and the cafeteria and auditorium on the top of the western boulevard; the last one being a structure that is projected from the street level down to the middle of the park. The architecture project that accompanies the fair integrates a 1000 metre^2 construction of three independent structures: an auditorium for a minimum of 150 people, a self-service cafeteria, exterior esplanade for 70 people and an information pavilion. The proposal links the auditorium and the cafeteria through a large staircase, which allows the seating area of the auditorium to be extended to the outside. This solution of a created amphitheatre permits the users of the cafeteria to watch the cultural activities inside the auditorium, while appreciating the views over the city from the outside or through the large window opening behind the stage. This auditorium not only hosts cultural events linked to the book fair, but also concerts / theatre performances that can be enjoyed from the outside when its sliding doors are opened during the warm summer nights. It later became titled as 'Sky Lounge' and reutilised as a high level club for special events in the park during the summer months.

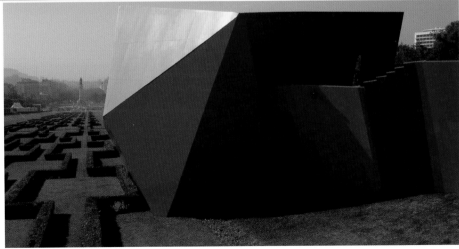

NURBSTER IV
SPLINEWALL TAIWAN

Developed in nine days by architecture students during the Feng Jia University 'Digital Architecture Design Unit and Workshop Exhibition', the exterior wall and roof are made of metal sheets; the interior wall constructed out of wood hosting a seating facility for animated projections on an incorporated digital screen.

Questioning traditional wall concepts and the interaction between users and the architectural skin, and observing animal features, translating them into possible digital constructs. Intuitive personal responses are transferred into abstract patterns and materialised using 3D software in a collective architectural piece.

NURBSTER I
LONDON & PRAGUE

The NURBSTER features enclosed vertical loops and singular horizontal stripes cut by CAD-operated machines out of standard-sized MDF boards. The pieces then formed a skeleton-like wall for the Unit 20 End of Year Show at the Bartfest 2004 integrating student projects developed in Japan. The NURBSTER adapts traditional Japanese wooden construction techniques of cut-joint fittings without additional fixings for quick assembly and disassembly.

A series of layered sections create a complex volume of NURBS (non-uniform rational B-splines) expressed through curvilinear and arabesque geometries that blur the boundaries between the horizontal and vertical frames.

arcos Cruz

arcosandmarjan?

olution conveys the various
the discipline), overlap
etc) and interference
le is, perhaps, exuberant,
rpolated and infiltrated by
olution and properties to
sign (CAD)—topology,

embodied flesh, which
cal depth to all our projects.
language instead of style,
spects, but also to issues of
lture, all of which create a
real and experiential values.
eam digital discourse that is
a three-dimensionality and
om the inside out.

cy. In a digital system, how
softness and the grotesque?

hose qualities in architecture.
ver, step-by-step we try to
hich it expresses something
permeate the geometries
es, which are often not easy
of work (and also drawings)
layered sense of codes,
convey a sense of intimacy,
as well as potentially being
grotesque and the ugly—
n architectural practices.
always been to push the
g and use of dots, lines,
at the same time exploring
or example, I think about
ailable five years ago, it
t had previously felt rather
ur expressive capabilities

ngage in the exploration
memory, vision, cognition,

hearing, touch and motor skills on the human side, which within CAD (I believe) transform into automatic, intuitive, mimetic and reflexive processes. I also engage in more computer-related issues such as performance, communication and interaction, which again give feedback to the former aspects as 'digital mimesis', 'poetic automatism' and 'symbolic bliss'.

Such an approach favours the formulation of *DigiTales*—digital narratives about the strange, other and alien as well as the familiar, intimate and contextualised—that discern (actually reveal) a whole series of events and haecceities within digitality beyond the usual aspects of techniques, technologies and technics. Techniques, here, are understood as process and method; technologies as scientific knowledge and applications; and, technics as skills and functions. This setup involves and invokes a plethora of arguments on the performance (understood both as task and as staging) of poetics in digital architecture.

These circumstances provide an alternative to the understanding and production of truly contemporary, innovative and progressive digital architecture. Does the convoluted nature of the subject matter not go beyond the functions of complexity and intricacy? Does it not invoke something ranking above beauty, elegance and smartness? Does it not evoke the sublime, the blissful and the mysterious, the grotesque…?

Q. Do you seek inspiration from other disciplines?

Marcos: For me, there are numerous sources of inspiration, especially in science and art. This includes the perspectival, spatial and ornamental complexity of the Baroque (and also, in some, Art Nouveaux), the narrative paintings of Hieronymus Bosch and installations of Louise Bourgeois, and, above all, the extraordinary creative richness and humanness of Bruce Goff's architectural oeuvre. Medical sciences and biology, however, continue to be the most important disciplines influencing and challenging architects today.

I remember a few years ago having a book in my hands about microscopic imagery of rubbish collected in the Atlantic seabed— incredible and exciting stuff! It filled my mind with visions and the hope that architecture could be much more than what we were used to experiencing. In those images, as well as imagery from other histology books, there was a sense of perfection and imperfection apparent, attained through an unimaginable level of geometric intricacy. At the same time, it implied a sense of awe and beauty—something that in our time seems to drive a lot of the contemporary digital production. I believe that biotechnology, in particular, is an emerging field that is challenging designers with our existing digital tools to redefine the procedural, technological and aesthetic parameters of architecture. I call it 'neoplasmatic architecture'.

Q. How is a digital play or experimentation different from pen and paper?

Marjan: Digital design is not detached from analogue design and research issues. CAD will not, and should not, replace analogue annotated sketches, drawings or scaled models (a fly-through animation does not replace an intelligent circulation system; a new script does not substitute typological and structural ingenuity; ultra-photorealism cannot stand for lack of originality). I disagree that an architectural digital project cannot be communicated and evaluated by 'traditional', analogue representational techniques and documentations. It has an additional set of criteria and strategies, however, which allow it to go beyond the analogue drawing.

Yet CAD is not identical / symmetric or analogous. If CAD were analogous to analogue design, there would be a similarity in function, but not in structure and evolutionary origin. Digital drawings perform and function differently, and I believe the similarities to be homologous—they exist in terms of structure and evolutionary origin. In terms of origin, 2D CAD has undoubtedly evolved from traditional line drawing, and 3D from traditional model making. In terms of evolutionary parallelisms, I see CAD rendering to be linked to the work of Piranesi, and Étienne-Louis Boullée's tableau, or to photography, since all 3D CAD software packages allow different ways of displaying digital space on-screen.

The similarities, however, do not necessarily exist in terms of function. Although CAD is commonly regarded as less technical and more abstract than generative techniques and CAD/CAM technologies, it nevertheless functions and performs within the parameters of a domain overpowered by *Technik*, albeit transcending it. On the other hand, the danger is to disregard CAD as replication and simulation of analogue models, reality, craftsmanship and building construction. Instead, it is about drawing a unique symbolic world through systems of signs and premonition, and prediction and strategy. It is about construction, representation and feedback. In its multiple presences (line, wireframed, shaded and rendered), CAD escapes and hybridises the dichotomy of concept / image, strategic diagram / pictorial vision, 2D drawing and 3D model. It convolutes thing / image, object / space and sketch / product, but most importantly it entails an organic spatial and strategic vision that includes materiality, atmospherics and use. Consequently, it can transcend Technik.

Q. The Nurbster series is continually evolving, firstly as Cartesian 'swiggles', later disjointed planes—how do you see these experiments continuing in the future?

Marcos: Our Nurbster series has had a gradual shift from more formally complex and sculptural pieces to slightly simpler but more easily buildable forms. The tendency is to grow in scale and apply the

experiences of smaller prototypes to larger-scale projects, as has (in part) already happened in the project for the Lisbon Book Fair, the museum extension of MEIAC in Badajoz and the Lofting House in Lisbon. In all cases, the complexity is more to do with use, structure and context than solely with the playful control of 2D-3D fabrication processes. But there are lots of new iterations to investigate that imply, for example, the combination of different materials, material thicknesses and also fabrication techniques. There is also much more to develop in terms of language.

Q. Have you experienced changes in the use of digital architecture in student production and representation?

Marjan: On a critical note, I have to say that I have noticed that many understand digital design as mechanics. You need to understand the common process and then you follow it. I cannot agree with this. My approach is less mechanistic and more of an inside-out approach, initiating the project by each individual's observations, sensibilities and skills—that's the way we also teach our Bartlett and Westminster students. Moreover, I see an enormous lack of historical knowledge and building knowledge, as well as structural knowledge: CAD has no gravity, and so this is how the new generation designs.

SHAMPOO

KOSTAS GRIGORIADIS
IRENE SHAMMA
ALEXANDER ROBLES-PALACIO
PAVLOS FEREOS

URBAN REEF

Urban reef addresses the problems of localised ground discontinuity and programmatic, physical isolation within a larger urban area. It proposes a highly-connected three-dimensional network of housing, integrated with commercial and recreational zones. Located in west midtown Manhattan, Hudson Yards act as an ancillary urban outlet providing infrastructural support to its surroundings. The site acts as a physical division preventing midtown Manhattan from connecting to the Hudson River. A lack of housing and a prevalence of institutional and transportation buildings create a hostile environment largely unused by pedestrians, lacking in ground-related activities that could motivate movement from central Manhattan to the Hudson River.

The aim of the proposal is to connect midtown Manhattan to the Hudson River pedestrian paths, as well as create an elevated network of connections between buildings for housing development. The primary strategy was to create an artificial ground on top of the rail yards that would regulate the building positioning at a later stage. Based on previous research on Maya hair dynamics, the design of this artificial ground would be generated and regulated by setting out a network of connections across the site that would then be optimised to create the circulatory system of this new ground.

The first step was to identify the location of all infrastructural nodes at Hudson Yards and its surrounding areas, including ferry terminals, local bus stops and metro stations. Additional nodes were placed at regular intervals on the High Line, as well as at the perimeter of Hudson Yards that would later form the entry points into the scheme. Further site research established the number of pedestrians passing through every intersection around the site, at a period of 15 minutes and at different times of the day. This information was linked to the nodes, with every node 'reading' the pedestrian count of its nearest intersection point and translating this number into a connectivity value. This initial network was optimised using Maya's hair dynamics engine, resulting in the creation of openings in-between this circulatory network.

The next step was identifying the openings or clusters in which to situate the buildings. The selection process took into account the number of housing units specified in the brief, the creation of the continuous elevated network and the minimal disruption of the train lines.

A script was used to relate the area of each cluster selected to the size and height of each building's vertical circulation core. A threshold value of 3,000m² (beyond which the cluster would split in two parts) ensured that all buildings were kept to a maximum height of 150 metres. After all of the vertical circulation cores were set out, a second script generated all of the elevated connections between the buildings.

The rules of this 'bridging' system connected each building with the two closest, the connections differentiating in inclination from level platforms to ramped circulation corridors. This enabled the placing of enclosed retail or recreational spaces, as well as open landscaping or green spaces within the network. When all of the connections were established, a 'filtering' process deleted all connections above 120 metres and preserved those below 80 metres.

A third and final optimisation inflected all of the vertical connections that supported bridges between 80 and 120 metres. This reduced them to the 80 metre limit. This would ensure that, for structural reasons, all of the links between the buildings, either merely circulatory or supporting housing, were kept to a minimal span. A different selection of clusters at the first stage of this process would mean that the proximity relationships of the horizontal links to the vertical cores, and to the degree of inclination of each core, would have to be rearranged in order to achieve minimal spans while preserving maximum connectivity.

Working to a brief of 3,000 housing units, the usual isolated high-rise building types found in Manhattan were replaced by a series of mid-rise buildings that incline to minimise structural spans and also interconnect so as to maximise the area available for housing development.

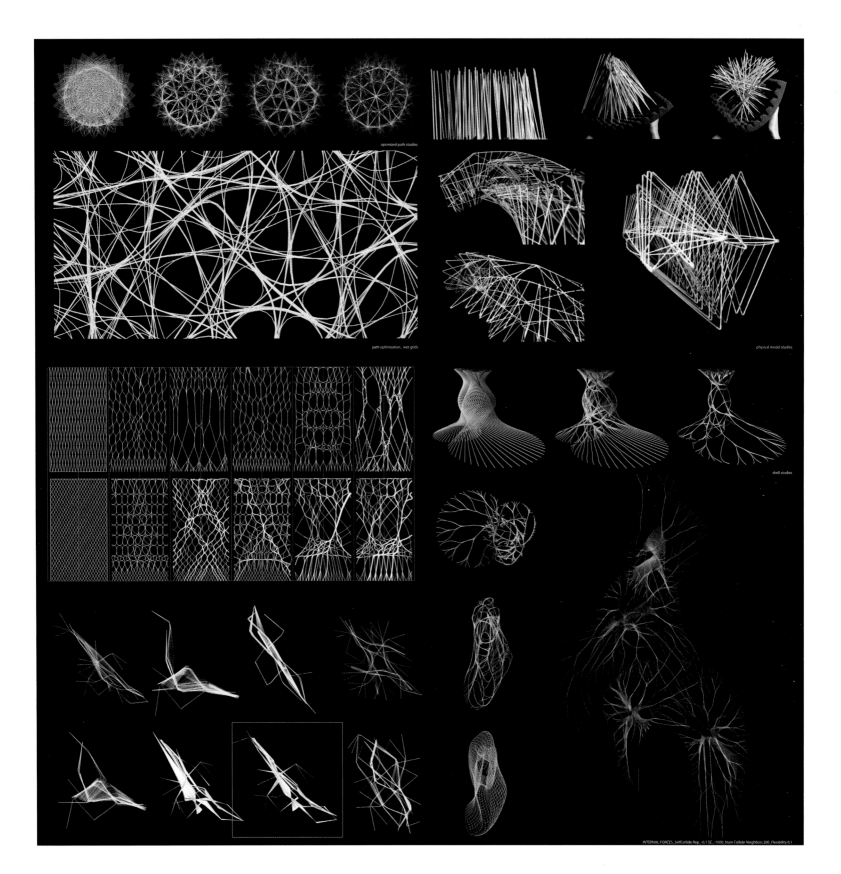

optimized path studies

path optimization_ wet grids

physical model studies

shell studies

INTERNAL FORCES_SelfCollide Rep_-0.1 SC_-1000_Num Collide Neighbors 200_Flexibility 0.1

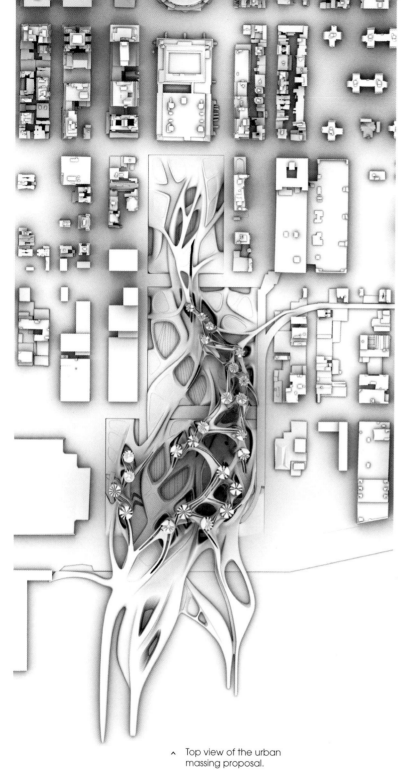

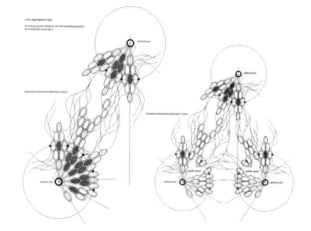

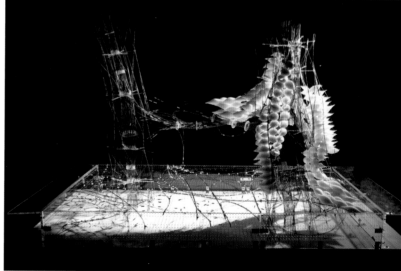

^ Top view of the urban
massing proposal.

^> Hair dynamics research studies,
virtual into an actual state.

> Working physical model of two
of the housing buildings and
their bridge connections.

< Hair dynamics research studies:
virtual into an actual state.

SELF SUPPORTING MEMBRANE TENSEGRITIES

Performative self-supporting membrane tensegrities, passive desalination and shoreline revetment—Hulhumalé, the Maldives

A tensegrity construction (without the use of wires), each individual unit has entirely intrinsic forces rather than transmitting to neighbouring units. Differentiating itself from conventional lightweight tensile design (which relies on heavy foundations to resist the forces and anchor the structure to ground), Toby Burgess's proposal relies solely on the capacity of membranes to transmit all tensile forces.

Through the integration of surface with structure, the amount of material in tension is maximised, reducing the overall mass. Through extensive physical and digital experimentation, using surface relaxation scripts and physics-based dynamic simulations, Burgess developed a catalogue of tensegrity units, described as 'simplexes'. Developed using Bentley's Generative Components, small variations within the multitude of membrane pieces dictate the global morphology.

Set in the Maldives, the project is a response to the threat of saltwater intrusion upon freshwater lenses. These shallow resources of water are the lifeblood of island communities, acting as a potable water resource simultaneously sustaining shoreline flora. The density of this vegetation is a fundamental natural defence against rising sea levels, reducing the impact of storm surges and major wave events, such as tsunamis.

With the very limited material resources of island communities, combating the effects of rising sea levels required the project to grow construction materials locally over time. In doing so, this enabled sustainable continued growth along the shoreline. Burgess's tensegrity system is deployed as a shoreline desalination device that evaporates seawater off the porous textile membranes using wind power alone.

The freshwater vapour created is harnessed by bamboo plants grown within the cooler interior of the structure. These cooler spaces reduce the evapotranspiration rate of the growing bamboo, and water not directly used by the plants falls to the ground and replenishes the freshwater supply.

The stems of the bamboo are used directly in the building as the compressive members. The bamboo plant is also used to create the textile membranes, which are woven from the softer parts of the plant. A tested industry that, although still in its infancy, could aid the local economy if developed and introduced.

The structure also 'grows' by a process known as 'biomineral accretion', which is the same process used by marine organisms to build skeletons, where the suspended minerals in seawater are converted into calcium carbonate or calcium silicate through organic processes. The membranes used are textile-based, woven from the bamboo grown onsite and with threads of conductive copper also incorporated into the weave. Very low-level electricity is passed through these elements, which, over time, causes the deposition of calcium carbonate on the structure. This process is currently used to build artificial reefs and results in a stony build-up similar in strength to concrete.

⌄ Physical model of system, testing shading potential.

UH: That's a good question. Making things a little bit difficult can sometimes be really helpful. When I was studying it was really hard to find a computer and so we had to hack things together, we had to sort of dumpster dive and figure out how to interface things to the computer in such a way that the final design was determined by the process of trying to find all these components.

Because these days there are all these tools that help us build these kinds of things, what I would hope is that we try to push further and further in what it is we are trying to do. Of course there still are things that are very difficult, and at an educational level those are the kinds of things I think we should be trying to do, because they make the brain be imaginative, overcome problems and not just do the same old thing that we see again and again.

One of the really useful things to do is to give a really good history lesson. I think when people realise the whole history of what they're doing, the impetus to go beyond that and explore new conceptual territory becomes that much more visceral.

1   *Amazing Archigram*—Peter Cook, Perspecta, (1967) Vol.11
2   Physical Computing's Greatest Hits (and misses) www.tigoe.net/blog/category/physical%20computing/176
3   Formula for Computer Art—Jim Campbell www.jimcampbell.tv/formula/index.html
4   The Architectural Relevance of Gordon Pask — Usman Haque, *4D Social Interactive Design Environments* (2007) Volume 77 No.4
5   The Wonder of Trivial Machines—Stephen Gage, *Protoarchitecture: Analogue and Digital Hybrids (Architectural Design Series)* (2008) Volume 78 No.4
6   www.pachube.com
7   www.arduino.cc
8   www.reprap.org
9   www.theoscarproject.org
10 www.openmoko.org

GEMMA DOUGLAS

UK HQ—BRITISH EMBASSY AND MINISTRY OF
DEFENCE IN THE THAMES ESTUARY

Real-time politics poses a question about the adaptability of architecture when security calls for immediacy. Will architecture leave behind Modernist principles of openness and transparency for the pragmatic and pressing task of safety and security? Should security be incorporated into architecture or be an add-on element? Should securing the built environment lie in the domain of the designer or specialist companies? While architecture's role was once to distinguish between the public and the private, it is something to console and manipulate. "There are very few monsters that warrant the fear we have of them," (Andre Gide, 1947).

The proposal's main concern lies in architecture's role in adapting to monitoring, protecting and defending what is being secured. A conceptual project on a fictional new island in the Thames Estuary explores notions of security, national identity and architecture's ability to both nurture and protect.

While central government is devolving power to local government, new citizens are being tested on the abstract notion of 'Britishness'. At a time when cultural identities are changing faster than ever before, are we encouraging diverse regional identities as well as an overarching British identity? Do we have to choose, or can Albion, a new island in the Thames Estuary, act as a region in the national interest within a diverse community? Can architecture help ensure our cultural survival?

A British Embassy in the UK explores the ambiguity and fluidity of Britishness, as a first port of call for new citizens arriving in the UK, alongside a relocated Ministry of Defence Headquarters. A seemingly picturesque and benign cross-stitched landscape simultaneously nurtures new citizens and secures a central government department encouraging assimilation and fertilisation of cultures. Heraldry is explored as symbols of nationalities in constant flux, expressed as a crest of landscaping and parking visible as you approach the UK by air.

Embassies are a representation of their people and governments—how can a British Embassy in the UK reflect a society in constant reconfiguration, with a tendency to nostalgically look back at a bygone era?

Cross-stitch, heraldry and the picturesque appear as distorted architectural elements, exploring reinvented familiar and nostalgic symbols of our national heritage recreating an old identity in a new place.

On the fabric pieces:

T.1,R
= Top chord, hypar number 1, Right corner of fabric

Variables:
Upper/Lower chord: U/L
Hyper ID: 1/2/3
End/Start/Left/Right E/S/L/R

On the overall location:
U2,0-V2,0
= U tile 2 and V tile 2
Variables:
UV Coordinates based on overall configuration

T.1,E T.2,E T.3,E B.1,E B.2,E B.3,E B.3,R

T.1,L T.2,R T.3,L T.3,R B.1,L B.1,R B.2,L B.2,R B.3,L

T.1,R T.2,L

T.1,S T.3,S B_ B.3,S B.2,S

T.1,S

U 0,1- V 0,1   U 1,1- V 1,1   U 2,1- V 2,1

U 0,0- V 0,0   U 1,0- V 1,0   U 2,0- V 2,0   T.1 T.2 T.3 B.1 B.2 B.3   U 3,0- V 3,0

U 0,3- V 0,3   U 1,3- V 1,3   U 2,3- V 2,3   U 3,3- V 3,3

U 1,2- V 1,2   U 2,2- V 2,2   U 3,2- V 3,2

0 years: 5% accretion   4 years: 24% accretion   8 years: 71% accretion

∧∧ Parametric coding system to facilitate construction.

∧ Tensegrity structure diagram illustrating electromineral accretion over time.

› Individual cutting patterns of fabric are generated from a global arrangement within generative components.

IN
CONVERSATION
WITH

USMAN HAQUE

Interview by Ruairi Glynn with Usman Haque

RG: Before we talk about your current projects, I wanted to go back to when you were studying architecture—what led you to the work that you do?

UH: I think that I have always been interested in systems and in the relationships between things. I've been less interested in necessarily physical artefacts, and I was never really good at evaluating form, justifying it or explaining it to myself. I always had this kind of intuition that the relationship between things was what I wanted to pursue: my relationship to space, my relationship to other people in space and how the system of the perception of space is actually a constructive act. So I'm actually part of a process of constructing my environments to the perceptions of it.

The moment of clarity for me was when I was sitting in my aunt's living room in Pakistan. In Pakistan, the middle class very often have servants, and so servants' quarters. I was sitting on the sofa surrounded by my family, talking and gossiping, and the servants were in their quarters off the kitchen. I started imagining how you might wire this place up so that there was a microphone in the living room connected to a speaker in the kitchen or to a speaker in the servants' quarters and I suddenly realised that this slight change would dramatically alter the space.

All of a sudden, for the servants, the things they do, the things they say or even the way they look at each other would perhaps change immediately. This tiny alteration of what I started thinking of as 'soft space' had everything to do with social structures, but it also had very much to do with the fabric of the architecture. It's not simply something that's overlaid; it's something that can actually be designed into the space, which I suppose was the moment when I started thinking about the ways in which you could actually reprogram space using fairly subtle interventions.

RG: I know that cybernetics was a big influence on you at that time and continues to be. Is the discipline something that you reach into to think about your design process?

UH: Definitely. The really important thing for me about cybernetics, or the value of it, was that it provided me with a framework to start to understand the kinds of things I wanted to design and build. It's a very rigorous framework with very specific definitions for things like interaction, perception and conversation, and the observer and the observation.

It also helped me to be able to evaluate what I was doing, to critique what I was doing and help to find ideas and situate what I was doing within a historical context. To that extent, cybernetics was very important early on and I would definitely say the work I am doing now follows in the same trajectory—although I don't tend to use the word cybernetics quite as much.

RG: Do you think that's because people are intimidated by it and often don't understand or misunderstand it?

UH: It's actually because I'm a little tired of explaining what I mean and I don't need to justify it. I use the strategies that cybernetics has in order to do things, but it's a word that people have all sorts of different ideas about and I'm not that intent on defending any particular position. And the same goes for the word 'interaction' and even 'architecture' to a certain extent.

RG: Peter Cook once suggested that we think of architecture not as a tight discipline, but rather "regard the city, or whatever replaces it, as an infinitely intermeshed series of happenings"[1], as apposed to just the provision of walls, roofs and so on. This seems to relate to your 'soft space' as an understanding of architecture where the relationship between things is as important as the physical nature of these things. Now 'interaction' is a very specific type of relationship between things, and it strikes me that few architects consider it much more than sensors triggering actuators of some kind.

UH: If we are talking about 'interaction', and very specifically what it means to me, what I tend to do is contrast it to the word 'reaction'. Whereas 'reaction' implies a certain degree of predictability and causality, 'interaction' is also deterministic. 'Interaction', however, is where the 'reaction' calculation changes, and 'interactive' is the way something responds to changes. Of course almost everything is reactive in a sense in that you flick a light switch and a light goes on. But the most interesting type of system for me is the interactive one where you flick a light switch and the light may actually come on—there may be a number of reasons for that, but what's important is that the program that connects the input to the output is not fixed.

RG: Over the past couple of years, through the course of exhibiting my work and writing on interactive architecture, I've seen a lot of objects, installations and architecture that I've found increasingly predictable—a repetition of certain basic interaction projects redressed in newer technologies.[1, 2]

UH: I would never say that there's anything wrong with doing these things, and certainly it's made sense in the past to work that way because our technical capabilities were not advanced enough, and our conceptual capabilities are also not as advanced. This is not trivial stuff conceptually to consider, and working on predictable reactive systems makes sense because they're really easy to debug. You know when they're not working and when they are working and you can start to figure out what's going on inside.

As our technology gets more sophisticated, and our conceptual frameworks get more sophisticated (which I do think they are), we are better able to start to deal with these complex systems. Wikipedia as a concept 20 or 30 years ago, for example, would have been almost impossible to process.

Now, it all starts to become clear, and I think that the kinds of systems that we can build in architecture, such as the interactive systems we are discussing, can also become clearer. It is very much to do with participative systems, the idea of being able to construct spaces that are not necessarily predictable. They might be deterministic, in other words you could follow the chain of causality through it, but they're not predetermined by a designer.

It is a really important thing for me in architecture—the considering of a spatial framework where the occupant, the inhabitant, the observer, the participant or the 'P individual' if you want to use the Paskian[3] word is the person who actually determines what that space is doing and how it responds to them. I think we can now deal with that kind of conceptual issue, so we don't have to just stick with our von Foerster trivial machines[4].

RG: When you talk about this framework, I think of those such as Yona Friedman's 'Spatial City' and Constant Nieuwenhuys's 'New Babylon', which I believe were suggesting Web 2.0-type strategies for our society, way before we built them digitally. And actually this notion of framework, which is very much an architectural principle, has been proven to work digitally perhaps much better in the virtual, than historically in the physical, and I do wonder how this may eventually lead back into the way we build our architecture.

For the moment, these social frameworks are being proven in the digital by open sources initiatives, particularly in software, but also hardware. And now your project Pachube[5] is really a part of this isn't it?

UH: Pachube is the platform, and it does fall quite comfortably, in my mind, in line with building massive participative architectural systems.

RG: It's a very smart strategy, particularly for small creative firms to take. You build up a framework and then you give it out to open source communities for them to harness the creative powers of masses as apposed to the few self-prescribed specialists. But before I ask you about Pachube, I'm interested in where you see open source models in architectural practice working? It's a subject that often falls on deaf ears with architects.

UH: I think when you introduce the idea of 'open source' to the discourse around architecture, there are two completely different routes to take. There is the route where you say that the design process or design tools are open source in some way. And the second is to say that the finished items or the finished entity is open source.

In my mind I don't think too much about the design process or the design tools, I'm much more interested in how the final structure can be considered as this kind of open participative system. You can start to think about what you might call the 'granularity of participation' in architecture. In other words, there are people who have the technical skills to participate at very strong levels of details, and those who will have the technical skills to participate at a level that others may not. If you start to think about having these different layers of participation, then you can imagine there are people who don't have technical skills who are also able to participate in the production of the space, so they are able to participate in the reconstruction of the space.

It's all a little bit non-specific, but what I am saying is that I don't believe that you should have a participative process during the design phase where you're basically doing a design by committee and then have a building that is unable to be changed. The whole point is to be able to design a building that is responsive to the people actually using it. And that's where open source as a strategy interests me most, because this has not even been solved in the software world. There are still discussions about it, there are still problems with the model, but that doesn't detract from the fact that there have been some pretty amazing things to come out of the open source approach in the software world and now in the hardware world as well. Things such as Arduino[6] and RepRap[7], the open source car (OScar)[8], the open source phone[9], and so on. Clearly, we are working these things out as we are going along—nobody has all the answers for open source and actually that's the point of open source. There have been attempts to do things in architecture with open source, some of which have actually been successful, others less successful. But we're getting there.

RG: What effect will this have on specialisation and on our profession? Is open source more suited to solving large scale problems rather than site specific ones?

UH: The important thing about open source (and, of course, in the software world there are a number of rules of what constitutes open source) is the fact that a piece of software is 'open', which means two things: one is that I can change it and the second is that I can actually see what it is. Even though open source software is used by millions of people, and only a few hundreds of thousands are actually changing it, doesn't detract from the fact that those millions of people can still see what's going on behind the interface. They might not understand it, but at least they're afforded the privilege of being able to have access when necessary to that software structure, and I think that is a very important thing to think about in architecture.

If there was an open source framework for architecture in the urban sense, I don't expect everyone to be putting on their builders hats and

going out there building shabby structures that will fall down. What I do expect is for there to be specialists that emerge from this kind of field and people to engage in DIY on their own home technological systems, because people will want to (and are already starting to) be able to access this. I'm very scared at the thought that Microsoft could determine how our houses are programmed and how they respond to us, because I don't think I will have that DIY capability if that is what happens. And that really is the point of the open source movement.

RG: There are only about six or seven firms that conceivably have the technical scale to be able to say, 'we can do TVs, computers, garage doors, the lot', and these are the likes of Sony, Apple and, Microsoft. They've all got big groups of people working on this idea of building an integrated, automated home. Apposed to that now are the various intermeshed community initiatives working in parallel but continually sourcing from each other. You talk about Pachube as potentially being able bring all these things together—where do you see it fitting into that home-DIY kind of attitude to rebuilding architecture?

UH: Pachube is actually supposed to be a platform, a tool with which people can build things. The reason why I launched it was because I saw loads of conversations about buildings being able to talk to each other, physical devices being able to use the web to communicate, to share sensor environmental data and so on. And all these initiatives seemed to be preparatory, closed and actually technically quite difficult for people to grasp unless you're an engineer.

I launched Pachube to start from the other side—what if it was an open system? What if you don't presume that buildings want to have a private conversation, but that they actually might want to talk to all the other buildings, share the data with all the buildings near by or with devices on the other side of the planet?

Essentially, Pachube became this kind of generalised data brokerage for object's sensors, interactive environments and buildings, enabling them to share environmental data in real time, but also facilitate not just one-to-one connections but many-to-many. That's not to say that you can't build private or secure applications on top of it, but it starts from a position of saying, 'let's actually have an open ecology, an open ecosystem kind of communication'. And the way I analogise it is, for example, when Nike and Apple collaborated to manufacture a shoe that had a sensor in it and it built up a kind of community around it. It actually made sense that they were able to do that as they are big companies with the infrastructure, web and hardware experience to web-enable a physical product.

But there's a huge number of small-to medium-scale designers, manufacturers, makers and DIY people who want to web-enable their products, services, buildings or houses, but there is actually no easy platform within which to do that. That's why we originally launched Pachube to say "let's make it really easy so that, while you need to be able to code, you can actually prototype the system with one line of code".

That's the most important aspect—you can see how it works with one line of code, test it and feel confident that it is working, while having a really clear development path to something that could actually work with existing construction industry standards. So you could build something in five minutes that does almost what you need, or, given more time, you can actually get something that can interface with the building management system, an electricity meter, a grid and so on.

RG: You've taught at the Bartlett (UCL) for a number of years and I'm interested in your opinions about the teaching of digital tools. Do you think that students should be taught how to code?

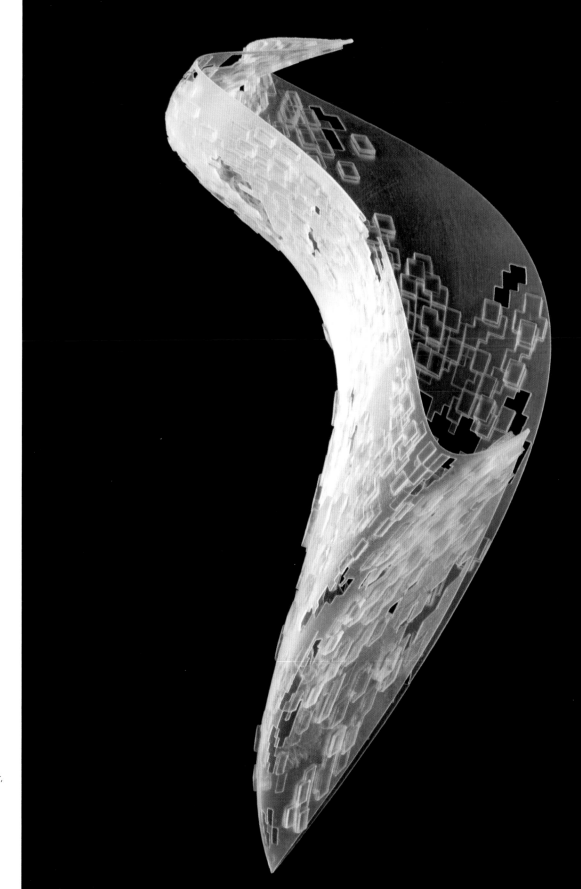

> Cross stitch, explored as a
nostalgic symbol of heritage,
becomes a three-dimensional
distorted architectural element,
protecting government
buildings from electronic leaks,
where the facade becomes
thickened surrounding high
security program.

‹ A seemingly picturesque
landscape forms car parking
and security features to
the Embassy. Landscaped
approaches nurture new citizens
towards specific entrances and
services, while lakes provide
security features. Car parking
is colour-coded and forms a
heraldic crest visible from the air,
as you approach the UK.

Sixteen*(makers) is a research-based practice bridging thresholds between the ideal and the real. Central to our approach is the production of speculative prototypes as a means to discover, accrue and adapt ideas for architecture, some of which begin as a hunch or curiosity, and others evolve into completed works. Over two decades we have amplified our repertoire as designers by an intimate understanding of digital and analogue manufacturing processes, time-based realities, responsive systems, environmental behaviours, and space that adapts to change. Our skills have evolved by adopting techniques from the hand-made to the digitally crafted through projects with an experimental edge that are widely published. Outputs range from buildings, installations, furniture and research constructs, as well as a diverse range of publications exploring ideas behind and around the portfolio.

Members include Phil Ayres, Nick Callicott, Chris Leung, Bob Sheil and Emmanuel Vercruysse. The practice is formed around mutual interests while individuals pursue parallel investigations in teaching, practice, research and manufacturing that guide our collaborations. Recent works include '55/02' (2009) a shelter in Kielder Northumberland, 'Assembling Adaptations' (2003–07) work from an elongated architectural residency also in Kielder, and Blusher (2001), an adaptive and responsive construct that toured the UK in a Crafts Council exhibition entitled 'Making Buildings'. The practice was formed in 1994 by Callicott and Sheil in Shoreditch London while students in their final year at the Bartlett. In 1997 both were invited back to teach and run the school's first entirely workshop based unit. Nick Callicott has since established steel manufacturing firm Stahlbogen GmbH in Blankenburg Germany with Kristina Ehlert. Following five years as Director of the Graduate Diploma/MArch Programme, Bob Sheil was appointed the Bartlett's Director of Technology in September 2009, where he runs Unit 23 alongside Emmanuel Vercruysse.

SIXTEE
(MA

55/02

55/02 is a collaboration in design and manufacturing between sixteen*(makers) and Stahlbogen GmbH. It is located on the north shore of the Lakeside Way in Kielder Forest and Water Park Northumberland, on coordinates 55° 11.30 N, 02° 29.23 W, the source of its abbreviated name. 55/02 explores the symbiotic relationship between design and making once central to the production of architecture and now rekindled by CADCAM, a disciplinary medium that binds the protocols of drawing with those of fabrication. 55/02 is made from steel that was cut, pressed, assembled and installed by a hybrid of digital and analogue techniques for which no final set of drawings exist. The relationship of the work to an ever more hybridised world, extends beyond the production of '55/02' as an artefact, it forms the basis of the architecture's layered relationship with its setting. It is a manufactured architecture in a manufactured landscape.

of revising drawings was quite a big deal. Now drawing, and thereby design, is a form of information that leaks between various states of certainty, representation and instruction. So when I said "Post-digital designers more often design by manipulation rather than determinism", I was arguing that a state of change and adaptation, rather than one of prediction has become common in design practice. But now that I have the chance to add to this, I would also say that I'm far more interested in parameters that are intellectually or conceptually driven than merely geometric.

Q Can you talk about how you consider the practice of making equivalent to that of drawing?

A We talk a lot about making, both in the unit and in the practice. What we don't often get the chance to say in print is that our attitude and approach to making has been arrived at through a foundation in drawing. When I first took up metalwork, it felt as was as though I was drawing in another material. For someone more versed in representing materials than working with them directly, the shift in practice imports understandings formed in a visual manner.

Thus the oscillation of three chemical states in welding steel for instance is a profound reminder of the materials transformable qualities. Thus we have always been aware that our attitude to making is established by an understanding of drawing and our position as designers, we just don't regard the paper drawing as the only product of the architect.

Q On to 55/02, could you expand a little on the project's response to site, what do you mean by a manufactured architecture in a manufactured landscape?

A Kielder Park is a confluence of opposing states; the man-made and the natural, the utilitarian and recreational; beauty and isolation, and weathers that converge from east and west. Forestry management techniques have evolved considerably since the 1920's when the first saplings were planted and harvested by hand. Now it is fully mechanised and digitised, the territory of 650 square kilometres can be designed for visual appearance. It is shifting from the utilitarian to the picturesque, upon a satellite coordinated mosaic. We find this transition fascinating and in designing '55/02' called upon our reading of the landscape as a mapping of artificial intervention. We were therefore keen that 55/02's form, configuration, orientation, scale, adaptability and materiality would form a connection with these events.

Q What advice would you offer young graduates today?

A Your education provides you with a broad base from which to challenge preconceived models of practice, research and discipline. Remain curious, flexible and willing to take risk. On the latter, especially early on, as the longer you leave it the harder it gets.

ADAM NATHANIEL FURMAN

THE CHURCH OF PERPETUAL EXPERIMENTATION

The project involves a sprawling new church in the southern Roman suburb of Esposizione Universale Roma (EUR), set within the fictitious context of a new pontificate that is devoted to the massive restructuring and expansion of the Church, its liturgies and its architecture (Vatican III). The site in EUR is set aside by the new pope as a field of experimentation, where the doctrinal and liturgical innovations being developed in the Vatican are immediately put to test (architecturally as well as liturgically) with the practicing and non-practicing public. The project proceeds over decades, as the Catholic Church develops experimental new architectures and ceremonies, while simultaneously developing techniques that allow this to occur on the same plot of land without erasing the elements of past experimentation. Developed specifically through a system of assemblage, Furman's work proposes an alternative architectural relationship to the contemporary paradigm of a discontinuous and fluctuating material environment. This technique of assemblage was explored and expanded on three scales:

The scale of the construction unit (or the assemblage of construction units);

The spatial unit (or the assemblage of spaces); and,

The compound unit (or the re-assembly of both construction units and spaces).

When linked together, the three scales (in time) helped to create a process of formal involution; a process that moves from the discrete spatial unit, to the juxtaposition of these units in the site, to the indefinite multiplication of their boundaries and, ultimately, to the formulation of a new and compound spatiality.

As an ongoing chain, this process or system can have new units assembled into it at any time, each of which, in turn, come apart and serve to enrich the site and its spaces with further formal material.

This exploration of assembly was an attempt, within a rapid and contemporary formal process, to recreate the manner in which the millennial palimpsests of our older cities and cathedrals carry the marks of every stage of their history. Spaces that have had the time to become layered with their own histories rarely have the opportunity to endure today, as buildings and urban areas are rapidly replaced in their entirety by an economy that demands continuous and wholesale change. Using the contemporary pace of urban transformation as a positive generator, the project set up its process of assemblage as a way in which rapid change can not only occur, but also be used to build up a formal continuity and architectural richness.

This is done via the transformation of an institution that, through the strength of its doctrinal narration and strict definition of architectural meanings, has always managed to powerfully combine diverse and discrete places, spaces, architectures and times. The project simply extends the natural tendencies of the church to an extreme degree, pushing their inventiveness, with regard to both architectural form and liturgical ceremony, into a velocity and level of experimentation on a par with that of the marketplace. This release of energy is then imploded into one, complex point (the site).

The complexity of such rapid experimentation and of what occurs onsite is pulled together using a strong and continuous form of narration, which defines the complex relationships between the architectures and their contents at any given point. This narration is substantiated in the story-telling qualities of the drawings, in the figurative nature of the models and in a separate film, and is treated as a form of critical self-consciousness within the work.

As well as the need for clear narration, the process set up by the project required a commitment to the use of both digital design tools and digitally-enabled fabrication technologies. The flexibility of these techniques allowed for the kind of fast-paced design process that the project required. They also helped in the reappropriation of traditional building materials from central Italy (travertine, maiolica, ceramic tiles and tufa), allowing them to be fashioned into almost unrecognisable forms and spaces. With that also came the freedom to explore certain aesthetic factors that might otherwise have been too time-consuming to incorporate, from texture and composition, to polychromy and pattern.

The role of image construction also changed from being just a tool for representation into being a whole area for exploration in itself, in which the project's spaces

> The models of various areas within the Church.

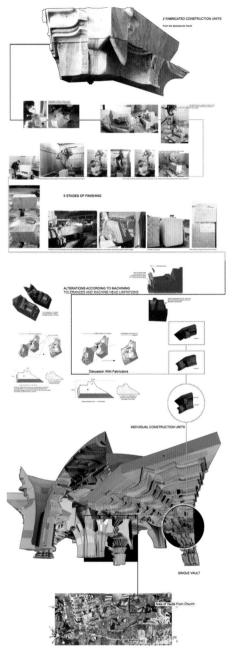

<< Stages of structural
development and exploration
for the church's vaulting.

< Description of the journey to 1:1
fabrication of two voussoirs from
one of the church's Vaults.

^ Close up of church vault model.

were probed and investigated as much as shown and
described. The same intuitive approach was developed
through model-making, drawing and video, and in each
of these mediums there was a continual pleasure with the
discovery that technology may be used in a manner that
creates a type of architectural space, which, using digital
design as a liberatory engine, was potentially richer and
more playful.

‹ Model illustrating various components of church.

› A model of a spectacular staircase pinnacle, where performances of spectacular mass conclude in one of the church's many sanctuaries, and over which the vaults reach a crescendo of articulation and polychromy.

PHILIP BEESLEY & METTE RAMSGARD THOMSEN

PROFILE

Mette Ramsgard Thomsen is an architect working with interactive technologies. Her research centres on the design of spaces that are defined by physical as well as digital dimensions. Through a focus on intelligent programming and ideas of emergence she explores how computational logics can lead to new spatial concepts. Mette's work is practice-led, and, through projects such as 'Slow Furl', 'Strange Metabolisms', 'Vivisection' and 'Sea Unsea', she investigates the design and realisation of a behavioural space. Her research focuses on the relationship between crafts and technology framed through digital crafting as a way of thinking of material practice, computation and fabrication as part of architectural culture.

Mette is Associate Professor at the Royal Academy of Fine Arts, School of Architecture, where she heads the Centre for Information Technology and Architecture (CITA). She has researched and taught at the Bartlett School of Architecture, the Department of Computer Science, University College London, and the University of Brighton, School of Architecture and Design.

Philip Beesley is an Associate Professor of Architecture at the University of Waterloo who practices experimental architecture and digital media art. His work in the past two decades has focused on immersive, interactive sculpture and landscape environments. He directs Waterloo's Integrated Group for Manufacturing, Visualisation and Design, and Riverside Architectural Press. His practice includes public buildings, development planning and interior installations. He has published a series of books on new technologies and innovative practice, including the recent titles: North House (CDRN 2008); Maison Solaire (CDRN 2008); Mobile Nation (OCAD, 2007); On Growth and Form: Organic Architecture and Beyond (Tuns, 2008); Hylozoic Soil (Riverside, 2007); and, Ourtopias: Cities and the Role of Design (DX, 2007). Press includes WIRED, Mark, Leonardo and AD features. Distinctions for his work include the Prix de Rome in Architecture (Canada), VIDA (Madrid, 2009) and FEIDAD (Taiwan, 2008).

CITA SUMMER SCHOOL

The summer school investigates how concepts of interactivity and responsiveness can suggest new ways of thinking of the relationship between the building and its environment. The contemporary societal context necessitates the thinking of sustainable solutions for our built environment. But how do these challenge the way we think and design space? How do we challenge our understanding of sustainability from being a set of posterior technological implementations to become part of the intellectual thinking and culture of architecture? Where formalist design traditions uphold the autonomy of the architectural artefact, we ask how ideas of interfacing and actuated behaviour can allow a re-conceptualisation of core architectural terms such as 'context', 'shelter', 'programme' and 'extension'.

The summer school asks:

If interactivity presents us with an inherent openness towards the exterior, how can new models of permeability and exchange challenge the way we think 'site' and 'enclosure'?

If embedded actuation allows for adaptable structures, how does this challenge the primacy of permanence in architectural design?

What are the technologies and materials that can enable the realisation of this new architecture of responsiveness?

What is energy, how can we harvest it and how do we exploit it?

The following text is an excerpt from a conversation between Philip Beesley, Mette Ramsgard Thomsen and Ruairi Glynn at the International Summer School held at CITA: Center for Information Technology and Architecture (August 2009).

PB: The architecture community is going through a wholesale transformation in practice. Taking very much to heart the 2030 challenge of equipping a new generation of designers with the skills needed for achieving carbon neutral cities and learning to integrate digital simulation with measure into our craft, I believe we should be working quite experimentally and not just filtering or applying an ethical sustainability of reduction to practice. I think we should be keeping it more generatively about what renewable approaches could be: capturing the cultural initiatives that would be so very motivating, creating viable systems rather than reducing and stopping.

I am curious about the subtitle of your book, *Passages Through Hinterlands*. It implies the gathering of marginal practices and distributive systems and speaks a step beyond the commonly understood tangent of the positivist, proud, powerful retooling that digital architecture implies.

In my own work, those values point to the use of tools that are specifically grounded in particular places, as apposed to warped into a universal system. I would imagine this book is pursuing some paradigms for interactivity and a cluster of relational models.

RG: We wanted the book to be rich in digitally enabled processes, but these must be rooted in some kind of individual agency and responsibility. There's a particular set of software and design paradigms that has bred a glossy rendered homogeneity to what I observe as the popular understanding of digital architecture. This book intends to look outside of this territory for the pioneers breaking the rigid constraints of such tools. We've looked for, and are trying to encourage, individual agency and responsibility.

That's what you're doing at this workshop. You've brought together students from all over the world to Copenhagen to think about these pressing social and technological issues. It's particularly different in a number of ways, not least because there's a dialogue with biologists and chemists integrated into it. This interaction of ideas is sometimes literal, sometimes metaphorical, but it feeds complexity into these systems we're constructing here, which is very admirable for a two-week workshop…

PB: Precocious let's say!

MRT: We're in a culture that is increasingly informed by highly engineered, high-performance materials, for example, the gasoline we put in our cars, the washing powder we put in our washing machines—they are all hyper-hyper engineered materials that are designed for the particular performance they are doing.

I find it inspiring to be in a culture that is starting to be able to grasp those tools and the interfaces that are allowing us to fabricate materials, either as our own customised composites or as new textiles where we make highly specified materials that are determine stitch by stitch. We can start to make new interfaces between architectural design space and these much more sophisticated fabrication spaces.

We are beyond this first digital paradigm of 3D modelling as the information container. That's not what it's about anymore; it's about the depth of the mathematics that lies behind it, and the possibility of symbolic calculation and what that actually means in our culture.

In the past five years, there are all these tools that are being developed that allow us apertures into the encoded parameters of these drawing packages. Of course, engineers have been working with these tools for a long time, but they've been closed away from our design space. There is a new depth to our design space arriving. At one level it's flawless and allows us to play the same tricks that we've played throughout classicism and modernism, but with more intelligence and complexity.

At the same time, however, it's actually a shift in the way that we relate material to representation. The drawing is fundamentally changed from something that is read to something that is instructing, whether a CNC machine or a chemical being manufactured. We've invited chemists and biologists here to participate, because it's just another scale of thinking about what the relationship is between what we are doing with the textile logic of this installation and what laboratories are doing developing hyper-defined material performance.

This workshop at CITA is bringing other cultures into our architectural context. It is through shared sensibility and the making of discussions such as these that our practice can find the next step. And we've found from our own practices that this can only be done through making. This is an opportunity, both for us and the students, to participate and get to know each other, to generate a community and share ideas. I think this generosity and a desire to exchange and collaborate is really wonderful.

PB: In the digital context, it is perhaps striking just how profoundly material our work here is. We're working quite energetically with virtual tools and simulations, but they're constantly accompanied by material trials in order to inform.

The result is a composite in which each of those media acts as a perturbation and a source for further enrichment. A cyclical loop of several different practices of simulation, conceptual, ethical interrogation, measurement, proof of concept trials, fabrication, working with jointing systems and equipping for mass fabrication.

This new generation has been brought up in a digital environment and can recognise quite a bit of homogeneity and a repeating set of vocabularies in, for example, digitally manufactured objects. A decade ago they were fabulously interesting… as a possibility.

It's striking to see how much information you can invest in these practices when you see something physically decaying at the same time—burning, vaporising or buckling under force, or being polluted with oxidation. These material involvements are a tremendous source of renewal and complexity. They're highly complimentary to the dry and visually privileged operations in the world of simulation itself.

JOHAN VOORDOUW

PRINTED AEDICULES

The 'Printed aedicules' project sought to design an annexed library for the Museum of Manuscripts in Tivoli. The museum is located at the Villa d'Este, a World Heritage Site. To ensure that the new library would not affect the medieval structure of the village, it was determined that the proposed facilities be moved to a site near the museum, but to a location that would not affect the heritage status of its parent institution. Situated on top of a crag overlooking the cascades of the Anio River, the library sits on the picturesque periphery of the town near the Ponte Gregorianna, one of the entrances into the old town and directly adjacent to a large plaza. The library was designed to contradict the existing environment, planned as an extension of the town. Nestling the river valley, it lightly appropriates the historic ruins of the Villa of Manlio Vopisco, while conversely inserting spaces into the existing residences. The museum is an architectural contradiction: while it is a response to context, it is also completely alien to it.

The library was expressed in a new digital mode. Rather than exploring the configuration of the library as a series of interconnected spaces on a 'building' scale, the project sought a spatial inversion—using a varied typology of shelves to define programmatic space, but to explore these spaces within the scale of a book. The pages and chapters are a means of expressing both physical and imagined spaces of the library. Using an interwoven combination of text, illustrations and SLS models, the project formed architectural space on and through the page.

The title for the project, 'Printed aedicules', reflects a dimensional interplay between two expressions of space, using the book to construct space on the page and the shelves as the formal hierarchies within the architecture of the book.

The term 'printing' is poetically semantic in the context of this project, but it is used to allude to manufactured craft—the way in which the project was made. The printing press, the production of hand-made paper, the etching of the plates and the process of making the binding of the book into a finished product defined a number of rarefied skills to form a text within a book.

Furthermore, the term 'printing' can be used at multiple stages in the book-making process: to print on, to print out and now through digital processes, to print SLS.

The library, therefore, represents a new manufactured craft. A new poetic emerges from the dualism between the digital and the analogue, the handcrafted with the digitally crafted and manufactured.

The second term in the title, 'aedicules', is spatially more important—the way the project was conceived. It reflects a continued examination into physical and perceptual spatial hierarchies.

Traditionally, the definition of an aedicule is two-fold: either as a small space, typically a shrine in a temple or domestic environment; or, flattened as an architectural frame surrounding a door or window. This definition was the primary inspiration for the project, forcing the library to adhere to a dualistic dimensional interplay.

Two-dimensionally, the project flattens the library onto the page. Three-dimensionally, it opens aedicules between the larger volumes of space that would hierarchically define the library's spatial experiences.

The library was conceived as an extension for the existing museum at Villa d'Este—the Museum of Ancient Manuscripts. Aedicular frames are often found in manuscripts, where they act as architectural elements framing both three-dimensional space and a narrative flattened as an image. While it is noted that manuscripts are not 'printed', it is the spatial characteristics that were of interest. Furthermore, a library's primary interest lies (with)in books and the notion of the page, to which both manuscripts and printed sheets are equally relevant.

Three-dimensionally, the aedicules were SLS-printed forming the shelves within the larger carved volume of the book. The shelves are the 'aedicular shrine' as it were, containing the library's purpose and defining both the physical and imaged spaces revealed by the library itself and through the experience of the book.

A number of books were made. The aedicules (library shelves) were modelled digitally alongside a secondary landscape form that provided the larger carved volume within which the aedicules rested. These nooks and undulations sequentially alter the spaces as one flips through the pages, morphing the shadows and the reader's point of view. The model was than printed using SLS, while the pages were each individually laid out and hand-cut to prevent the burn typically associated with laser-cut drawings. It was this continual oscillation between digital modelling and

> The Paper Trail Atlas made physical what would conventionally be drawn on the page. It indicates the route by which paper travelled from central China in 100 B.C. towards Europe, reaching southern Spain via North Africa. It is therefore a loose representation of chronology, geography, history and context for the project melded into a single didactic form.

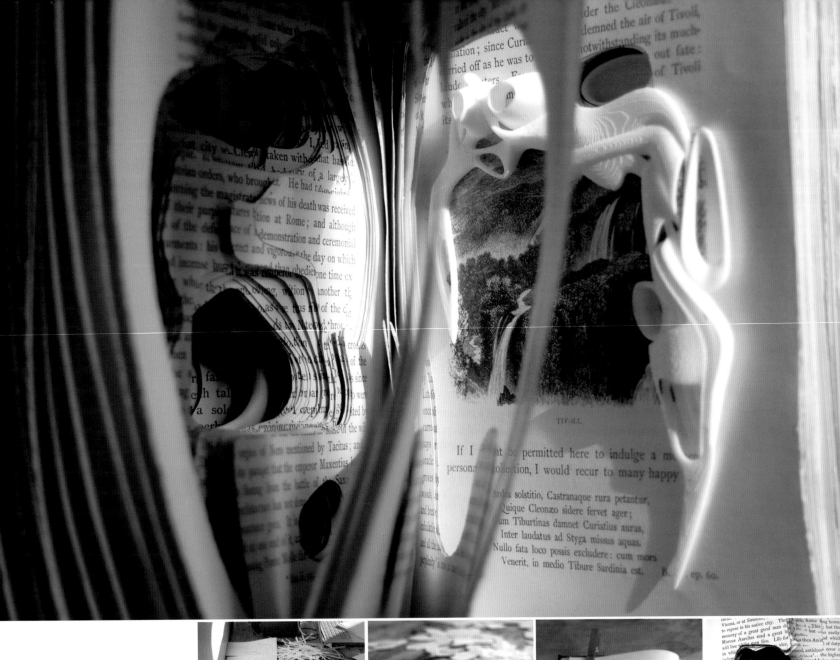

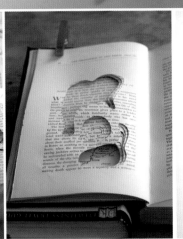

< ˅ 'The Pilgrimage of the Tiber'. Written in 1873 the book's text and images served as the context for embedded SLS models. The mapping sought to connect ideas, linking the map of Italy in to the etching of the cascades of Tivoli, using the text of the pilgrimage and hierarchically lifting them from the page, inverting and converting text to image, words to spaces and architectural forms to maps, using form as a means of heightening the expression of information and linking previously distanced ideas, and places through the page.

> The collage is a means of mapping both process and a number of various streams of information into a single drawing. It connects various scales of geography with schematic sections and perspectives of the library to form a new way of reading the project, and understanding concurrent links. It acknowledges that varied strands of thought are interwoven throughout the project and that this means of design development cannot and should not be separated or viewed in isolation.

˅ A line drawing of the interior view of library.

Map of Central Italy

Tivoli Site Plan

Central Axis - Library

Partial Section - Library

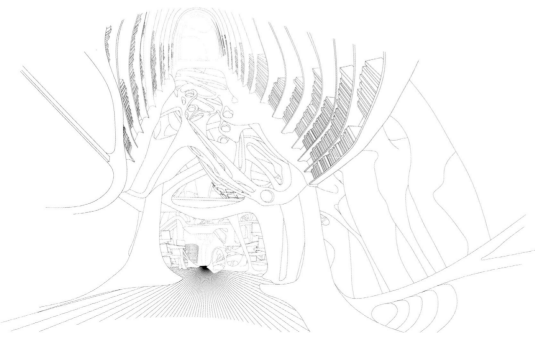

Hugo's visceral dislike for classicism went as far as for him to state that in actuality the European Renaissance was "that setting sun all Europe mistook for dawn".[25] Hugo felt that "Medieval buildings display "the imprint of a happy spirit"[26] and that the treatises "destroyed architecture's vitali... originality and local variety."[27]

handcraft that formed the basis of the project, finding a new means of manufactured craft. The process was integral to the theoretical concept, the dimensional interplay and the varied modes of spatial conceptions. The handcraft forms the context for the digital work. The SLS models are not constructed in isolation, but they sit embedded into architectural history, into meaning and into a new way of understanding architectural expression.

∧ The Printed Aedicules book is a composite of the previous works, however it has developed to articulate both the context and the content. It expresses a new mode of spatial inversion, exploring the physical and cognitive experience of a library through the scale of a book; as reading the book becomes synonymous with reading the building. These experiences form an oscillating interplay, blurring the boundary between the two and three-dimensional, the digital and analog. The SLS models woven into the pages express a cross-section of the varied shelving aedicules that articulate the spaces within the library. They are the spatial hierarchies that one flips towards and once reaching them, and peeling them over, reveals a new space, a new library one that contains all the physical and cognitive endeavours that should be explored and elicited through a new digital architecture.

MAYHEM

JULIAN JONES
RAFAEL CONTRERAS
MATEI DENES
DIEGO RICALDE

CRACKOLOGY

Julian Jones, Rafael Contreras, Matei Denes and Diego Ricalde (Mayhem) collaboratively focus on creating relationships between infrastructural flows and architectural space. They describe their work as moving beyond the traditional understanding of cellular space and continuous flows to create a new ground condition that exists between the two.

Using the principles of generating space through applied forces, their urban proposal 'Crackology' sets up a new sectional relationship to the city. Connecting this city, Mayhem's strategy is more complex than path optimisation; movements between connection points are parametrically formed using mass and trajectory of forces. These organisational principles lead to an urban strategy based on local parameters affecting larger scale urban flows.

The proposal for central São Paulo is in marked contrast to the linearity of existing city infrastructure. Flows are variegated, moving between private and public in a continuous pattern. Mayhem responded to the city's uneven and rugged topography (its deluxe developments standing side-by-side with its shanty towns) and its crude infrastructure by harnessing the Brazilian's unique ability to claim the interstitial spaces of the city for public interaction.

Using the computational properties of *voronoi* and continuous surface algorithms, Mayhem created a filtering machine for flows. As cars, buses and pedestrians pass through the site, their movements create an urban massing that is fluid to allow for a range of programmes from residential and commercial areas to office towers and a bus station. The focus of the work was on the public space created between these traditional programmes to allow for the spontaneous activity that is characteristic of São Paulo.

The *voronoi* cellular subdivision for the proposed layers of the urban park was produced by deploying a coherent distribution of points informed by the flow of a range of parameters, including traffic and pedestrian movement. Density of flows controlled the undulation and thickness of the surfaces creating spaces between the layers. The subdivision of the surfaces, obtained through use of the *voronoi* approach, provided a natural gradient in the overall pattern, and simultaneously the possibility of controlling the porosity / connectivity between levels.

For a proposal of this magnitude, a solution on a local scale was needed to provide the materiality and build-ability logics of its parts. Spaces were subdivided through analysis of the curvature and the concave-convex condition of the input geometry generating the final internal subdivision of the geometry, again using *voronoi* techniques. A structural framework was generated from the optimisation of edge thicknesses between subdivided geometry, resulting in a porous structure that, like the porosity on an urban scale, allows for visual and physical connection of differentiated spaces.

< Urban Blending.

^ Urban Proposal Global Scale.

DARREN CHAN

THE AERO FILTER

Examining the generative evolution, mutation and reorganisation of a city under the pressure of urban density, Darren Chan's 'Aero Filter' suggests high-rise solutions, using biomimicry on a colossal, scale to tackle pollution and the energy crisis. Focusing on the dandelion clock, Chan examined the seed-head sprouts of the pappus array, commonly known as 'parachutes'. The dandelion's highly efficient lightweight pappus and long stalk maximise the reception of wind, while simultaneously creating an air pocket between the parachute head and the seed head, resulting in a wind pressure differential, increasing the forces applied to set flight to the pappus.

Set in Bishopsgate, London, a parametric model was built to design form, structure and space using the understanding of structure and systemic elements. The structure takes advantage of a complex wind pattern created by currents that sweep around the adjacent cluster of high-rise buildings and funnel through the intersection of several thoroughfares towards the centre of the site. A distributed farm of micro-turbines is deployed along the diagrid nodes to assimilate ascending air flows. A series of particle dynamics simulations revealed distinct zones of turbulence along with pockets of low wind activity that were mapped in a gradient field to determine locations that would offer protected access to the building. Throughout the tower, open landscape and living zones alternate within a layered, striated double-hull morphology.

Strategies

In the pursuit of cleaner energy and less reliance on fossil fuels, the Aero Filter uses a skin of vertical wind-turbine arrays mounted on an external structural frame. The orientation and positioning of the turbines across the skin were dictated parametrically using wind data maps. The stronger and more persistent the wind in a certain zone along the skin, the denser the number of turbine modules became. These were prototyped using maxscripts (such as, meshscatter, randomselect, surface contour and greeble).

Using the London wind maps database, Chan derived data to maximise wind reception at specific altitude levels, responding to variations of directional wind strength around the immediate site boundaries. In addition, particle flow studies were employed to gain valuable information on optimal orientation, location of structures and form on site. The simulations specifically calculated and analysed patterns of how wind would most naturally ascend the building volume.

Chan argues that the implementation of hundreds of small lightweight wind turbines on a massive scale could be instrumental in resolving energy issues and restoring energy to the surrounding low-rise density buildings. A combination of material, formal and programmatic strategies was also employed, tackling the fact that density increases air pollution. A coating on the buildings external structure in TX Active (titanium dioxide) attracts impurities, neutralises harmful particles and also washes away harmlessly. Finally, the spiralling structure, populated by residential units, has vertical sprawl green spaces intended to naturally purify air as it is channelled through its strategic openings.

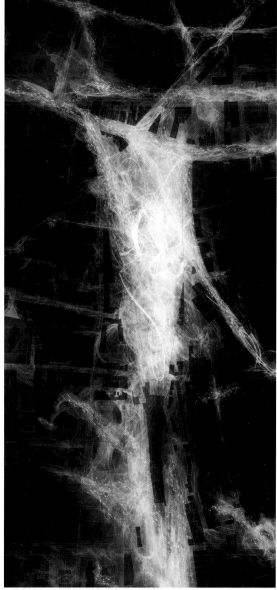

‹ Precedence.

› IMPACT "Visualization"
Realisation of the Aero Filter.

» DATA "Wind Simulation"
A detailed study of the site using
particle flow and wind data
map studies.

HORHIZON

RESEARCH BY DESIGN
WORKSHOP 03

BEN COWD
BRUCE DAVISON
TOBIAS KLEIN
DIETMAR KOERING
JUSTIN LAU
SARA SHAFIEI
EVA SOMMEREGGER
KENNY KINUGASA-TSUI
JOHAN VOORDOUW

PROFILE

Horhizon was established in 2008 as a research by design network, bringing together individuals and associations across various disciplines to create and conduct research themes and topics. The mission is to generate a wider architectural discussion and bring forward new and emerging fields of theory and architectural expression. Its members are located across Europe, establishing academic links that develop and articulate new modes of making and lines of thought.

Horhizon doesn't attempt to establish a singular line of research interest or methodology, rather it has formed an understanding of the diversity of digital interests ranging from the expressive computational to the digitally poetic and the poetically filmic. Its boundaries are rigorously inclusive and its expressions diversely crafted. Horhizon attempts to express new ideas through text, images and experiences, and recognises architecture's steadfast position in the physical, using the digital to explore a newly emerging spatial realm.

Urban Scenario Workshop.

Architectural Association, London. Students: Antonis Papamichael, Graham Smith, Stravros Papavassiliou, Huida Xia.

HORHIZON WORKSHOP OBJECTIVES

Horhizon has conducted a number of workshops across Europe. The intention of the workshops is to bring a new digital understanding into academic institutions, introducing students to new modes of process and design articulation. The workshops reflect an increased interest in computation, however, as the brief articulates, they are balanced with an intrinsic interest in spatial expression, theoretical rigour and architecture's physical presence.

Each workshop is a unique endeavour, developed to a finite end, whether that is teaching students new digital programs or modes of making and developing lines of theory. They are fields in which to experiment with ideas and test new technology, and the short duration of the workshops forces immediate participation. The intuitive forms a new sense of reason pushing students to remove pre-conceived notions of design with tangible response; each thought manifests into a digital expression. This playfulness often produces poetic results, as the freedom to pursue *via* open means conversely develops clearly defined architectural interventions.

This exploration further develops the Horhizon member's line of thought and modes of expression as the work conducted in the workshops is reinterpreted, articulating and inspiring the network's future work. This direct relationship reinforces the feedback intrinsic to the computational. The work is consequential because the workshops continually develop throughout the process of the brief and the students' design. Through continual re-forming, teasing, morphing and articulating, an architectural intervention is developed. Nothing is considered final as the workshop is an introduction—a preface to the students' own continued development in the digital.

As an academic research by design network, these workshops are fundamental to the mode of being, to further the nature of digital architecture and to see computation and craft not as a singular path forward but as an expanding field to be developed and propagated.

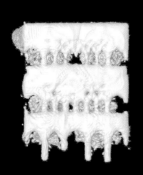

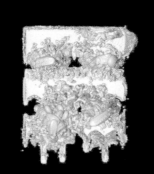

URBAN SCENARIO

Architectural Association, London
25th to 30th March 2009

Horhizon members:
Ben Crowd, Bruce Davison, Tobias Klein, Dietmar Koering, Justin Lau,
Sara Shafiei and Johan Voordouw.

'Urban Scenario' was a five-day workshop aimed at designing an architectural cinematic response to a possible London flooding scenario. Set along the river Thames, students utilised a number of monumental buildings to create a narrative architectural response to the brief. Students explored various tools of digital design and representation, and were guided by one-on-one tutorials, as well as lectures and software lessons.
    The main drive behind the workshop was to enable students to freely use complex 3D software in order to express narrative-driven digitally-enabled architecture. The workshop allowed students to cross-breed between various 3D representational software and actively encouraged the transfer between different tools of representation. This ensured a maximum degree of design freedom in response to the given scenario.
    Working in groups of two or three, the students had to develop and envisage an architectural intervention using an existing digital model of London. Students were able to create original, innovative and speculative architectural intervention using advanced visualisation and modelling packages, such as 3D Studio Max, Modo, z-brush, Final Render, V-ray and Rhinoceros.

DIGITAL DREAMLAND

University of Brighton
5th to 9th January 2009

Horhizon members:
Ben Cowd, Dietmar Koering, Justin Lau, Kenny
Kinugasa-Tsui, Sara Shafiei and Johan Voordouw.

The main objective of the workshop was to explore digital poetic narratives within the familiar context of popular film. Run over a five-day period, students were introduced to several 3D-modelling programs and encouraged to balance work in the digital medium with haptic investigation through the use of models.
    By way of recording, re-creation and re-contextualisation, film creates, defines and re-creates our future, present and past memories. For this reason, it was proposed as a powerful setting from which to manipulate, annex, intensify, elucidate, decipher, depict and design a speculative response. The workshop proposed that the tools and techniques originally used to design a filmic space can be reintroduced, and in doing so leveraged to imprint a secondary layer of experience and ultimately an evolutionary reading or future.
    Students were asked to choose snapshots from popular films as the basis for their explorations. By manipulating familiar scenes, or the 'ready-made', they were able to achieve a rich emotive ethos by leveraging pre-contextualised settings from which to construct their imaginative intervention(s). Working in groups of two or three,

they were challenged to learn and adopt various software platforms including Rhino, Cinema 4-D and Z-Brush. While the teams produced a range of digital and physical models, the exhibition primarily showcased the printed, re-imagined frames.

THE POETICS OF FLUID DYNAMIC

Ecole Spéciale d'Architecture, Paris
4th to 6th September 2008

Horhizon members:
Justin Lau, Kenny Kinugasa-Tsui and special guest Filipa Valente.

The aim of the 'Poetics of Fluid Dynamic' workshop was to investigate the topographical conditions of Venice and produce 'hydro-ecological' designs that would intervene with the water landscapes, wildlife inhabitation and urban conditions; as well as social and economical factors of the proposed sites.
    This three-day workshop included a fluid dynamic simulation seminar, allowing students to explore the techniques of fluid dynamics in architectural design, as well as a presentation given by invited guest, Filipa Valente.
    Students worked in pairs to explore the brief primarily using Real Flow, as well as 3D Studio Max and Rhino. The knowledge gained from the workshop stimulated students' sensibilities towards the material and psychological behaviours of fluids. They produced projects ranging from water / human interface designs, to the aesthetic productions inspired from the mysterious qualities found in fluid, such as material formlessness, grotesqueness, stickiness and spiritualistic sublimes.
    Each project used a wide range of digital mediums, such as film, drawings, renderings and CADCAM rapid-prototype models. Various projects have been published in the school's publications and featured in the online project archive of www.horhizon-paris.com.

MANUFACTURED SPACES FOR THE MOVING IMAGE

London, RCA, ADS1
25th to 29th November 2008

Horhizon member:
Eva Sommeregger

'Manufactured Spaces for the Moving Image' was a five-day workshop at the Royal College of Art for to the students of ADS1. It included lectures, software introductions, group tutorials and final crits. The workshop's aim consisted of rethinking architecture as a construction of perception—the architect / camera is part of the scheme, shaping it by viewing from a specific point of view, at a specific point in time. Students were introduced to digital film via the so-called '2½D' technique, consisting of a refined layered-up combination of Photoshop, after effects and audio editing
    Post-modern hyperspace's capitalist society works within different speeds of production—signs, signifiers, simulacra and real virtualities rule. Space becomes scape. Digital film is believed to be able to cope with this accelerated mode of production, and the workshop suggested

opening up towards a realm of perceptive construction of possibilities, rendering them visible and believable to the viewer's eye. In particular, how the ubiquity of imagery (and, specifically, how the moving image) changes and how architecture is consumed at the moment and consequently projected into the future.

Students were grouped into teams of two or three, allowing them to locate the film between the cornerstones of their personal year's research topic. They were asked to choose an aspect from the site of their year-long project and create a filmic scene from it. The narrative aspect of the filmic response to the site, as well as the compositional freedom, was key to the development of their scheme, allowing the students to project and construct a narrative space to engage with the existing and virtual site conditions. This was achieved by producing a layered up image in Photoshop and setting up a 3D scene from it in after-effects, allowing refined camera movement and audio linkage.

TOBIAS KLEIN

SYNTHETICS

Within the framework of the digital debate in architecture —currently often only led from a tooling and generative algorythmic point of view—the works soft immortality and synthetic syncretism try to form a post-digital idea, exploring the paradigm of a narrative 'inside-out' space. These projects argue for a re-evaluation of a digitally driven spatial definition that primarily focuses on the condensation of virtual into actual embodied within a narrative environment.

This space is clearly located outside the realms of digital objectivity and scripted optimsation. Rather it embraces design authorship that promotes the use of digital tools to sustain a synthetic architectural approach oscillating between a virtual and an actual, the poetic and the technological culminating with the condensation of narrative experiential qualities within n-dimensional spaces.

Soft Immortality

Soft immortality explores the idea of a digital embodiment, questioning the common representations of the body in the digital realm as a series of surfaces and layers. It creates a potentially new status where the modulation of the body's inner and outer surfaces becomes irrelevant. By using advanced medical visualisation techniques as both method and tool to redesign the body with variable intensities of matter, the obsolete notion of a finite body is exposed in favour of a new type of body-space that is, above all, a viscous field of variable concentrations of mass and matter. This creates an inverted design approach using a rigorously changed understanding of virtual space in order to transform the author's physical body into a hybrid data-driven soft construct within a seamless density modulation.

Derived from the use of non-invasive medical visualisation techniques (magnetic resonance imaging) and voxel-based presentation techniques, it attempts to reverse engineer the understanding of the body within the emergent immersive environment of a virtual continuum. The body is dissected, projected and analysed in a gradient of density fields generated from the MRI scans. The dissolution of the body's anatomical boundaries allows the reconsideration and recreation of it as a new physical territory in constant flux and change.

The resulting images are composed of a number of spatial frequencies at differing orientations where 'space' is

› Havana, Cuba—The necropolis Christobal Colon, the main cemetery with its iridescent marble figures, celebration and ritual of the syncretic santerian religion is the starting point for a journey deep in the grey areas between a condensated virtual into a narrative actual.

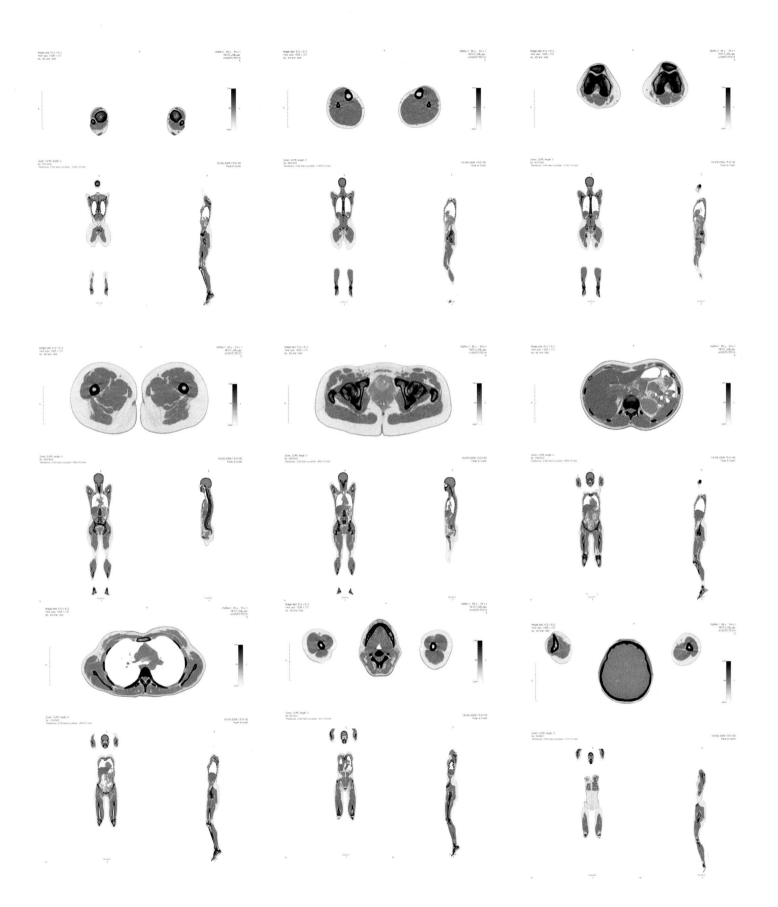

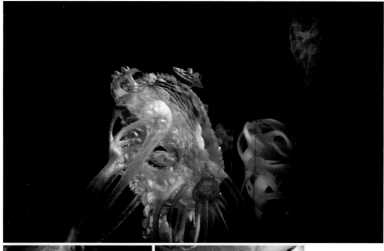

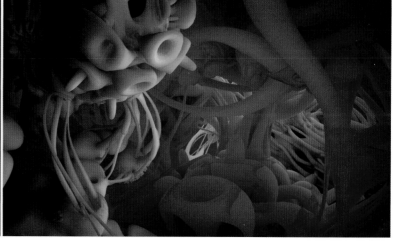

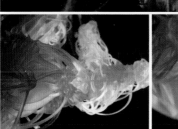
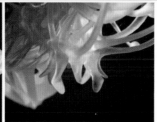

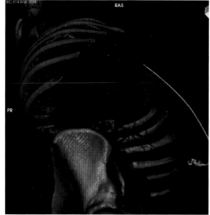

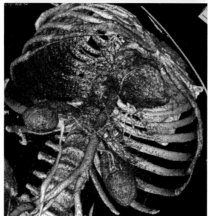

< The body as a complex spatial site that seen through non-invasive technologies becomes constantly in flux and without actual boundary but a construct of voxel-based shifting virtual flesh. Site analysis—series of body scans using CT showing vertical and horizontal sections.

^ Suspended split field condition that bridges the ontological slice of the CT scan and the viscous state of Magnetic resonance to form the syncretic transplant; a hybrid state between evert organ and immersed field.

> Raw data of a human MRI (magnetic resonance imaging) scan is taken as a starting point. Digital processes are used to create three-dimensional images from the inside of the body, as a result of interactive static and variable gradients of magnetic fields.

generated through interlocking density fields. Furthermore, MRI scan data is then used to reinvest a newly-created structure of virtual organs, permitting the emergence of a visceral state of poetic fluctuation between real and virtual flesh components. Virtual organs are redesigned as syncretic transplants, exploring a visceral state of fluctuation between real and virtual flesh components. These are hybrid natural-artificial mutations within newly created viscous bodies, ultimately leading to a transformation, from a Euclidean-described solid body to a field of informed particles, described in medical terms as voxels, it delineates new typologies of viscous bodies that are constantly readdressed, adjusted and, ultimately, modified.

Soft immortality is set within the seamless transitional fluctuation of a real / virtual body of Klein himself, an extended and projected body, where the traditional dichotomy between inner and outer space is dissolved. The human body acts as a catalyst to create immersive spaces that question our understanding of beauty, ugliness, voluptuousness and the ornamental within the amalgamation of digital technology and poetic notions. Ultimately 3D printed, soft immortality reassembles digital embodiment and creates a reactive field space. It oscillates and translates between actual physical and virtual constantly altering and avoiding a conventional framing and categorisation within one medium.

Synthetic Syncretism
Synthetic syncretism is the narrative application and further embodiment of soft immortality within a defined cultural and religious environment. Similar to the described voxel-based MRI-space, the dualistic concept of medieval soul-space, as well as site specific ritual-cultural-religious space are key elements in the transformation and development of a narrative based argument in a digital discussion surrounding an inside-out design approach.

The project's narrative background is based upon the hybrid Cuban religion of *Santeria* (a mixture between Catholicism and the African Yoruba tribe beliefs). As a result of this unusual syncretism, an altered kind of religion

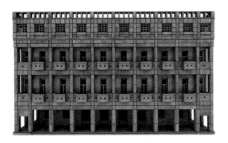

a - a

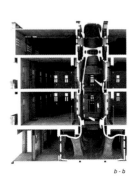

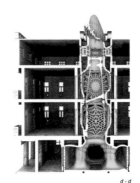

b - b   c - c   d - d

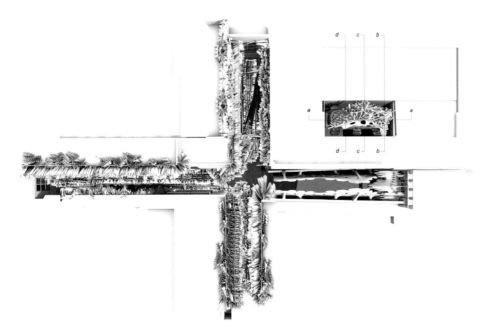

evolved that hybridises Catholic Saints with animals and *Sakralraum* with sacrifices to create a series of hybrid relicts culminating in a chapel along the procession route from the Necopolis de Christobal Colon to the shores of Havana, Cuba.

The surreal necropolis, with its richly symbolic figures and the equatorial sun scattering over the meaty marble of the catholic saints, is the starting point and inspiration of this proposal. The overwhelming richness of figurative marble catching the light makes them alive in a dead way. While the form stays the same, a womb-like life is created from within the figures.

Within this defined ritual space of the Santarian syncretic religion, the project artificially condensates the remains of sacrificial culture into a virtual hybrid, more commonly described as a relict. To create these hybrid relicts as spatially consistent structures it was necessary to immerse the physical into the realms of the virtual. For that purpose, similar to the process of a magnetic resonance image, the geometry of the physical object is scanned. At this point of the process, the object has become dual in its nature, able to carry, breed and later even extract parts of itself and/or added geometries of pure virtuality into the real.

The shaped and moulded object that is symbiotically connected to the immaterialised geometry of the bone becomes the organ of a larger entity. Objects can no longer belong to one perceptive medium as they flirt with the virtual and have an inherited longing for their expression into reality. The ornament, as a miniature without scale, becomes a celebration of the inherited urge to be moulded, shaped and connected to its host medium; the reality. These hybrid objects can no longer be processes of architectural imagination as they have to be materialised into the real. The hybrid construct of a church that presents one of the most important spaces in our history is becoming surreal as it turns into a hybrid object itself.

Soft immorality and subsequently synthetic syncretism no longer follows pure abstract algorithms or complex shapes created from scripted parameters. The temple is no longer distorting reality; it is reality that has emerged out of the ritualistic narrative virtual.

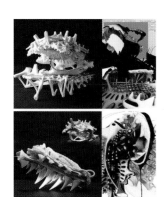

<> The Chapel of Our Lady de Regla, slotted inside an existing courtyard does not to imitate the algorithmic instances of intertwining elliptical shapes of a geometrical renaissance, but creates a protest against the white sober space of the modernism by reinstating the medieval dualism of our perception.

^ The ontology of formal creation starts as the dualistic site of the once-found physicality turns into a field of spatial possibilities. We enter the process that involves the total projection of the creator's mind to a virtual environment of data related sites. These relics are constantly in an oscillating state between actual and virtual and ultimately condense virtual into an actual state.

PATRICK USBORNE

MATARC

Increasingly, new universities and research clusters are touted as campus cities. The impetus behind such claims is the desire for the campus to draw upon the vitality of the city—to fuse together housing, research, culture and leisure components in an environment that attracts the brightest and ablest, ensuring the economic viability or survival of the expanding city. MatArc tackles the segregation of Paris's peripheral suburbs to the city centre by focusing on an existing city campus at the end of the Axe La Historique.

In 1964, Nanterre campus was envisaged as a utopian centre of education; a campus city, a punctuator, which would promote growth, creating a self-sustaining centre on the periphery of Paris. The campus city became engulfed within the sprawl of Paris, preventing the campus from becoming a punctuator for growth.

Nanterre is positioned at the end of the Axe La Historique, along which are a number of urban centres, from the tourist centre of the Arc de Triomphe to the business centre of La Defense. One characteristic they have in common is the monumental arch. Traditionally established at the end of a view, the monumental arch became a centre in itself for growth. This, in turn, connects it to neighbouring centres forming a web-like urban fabric, an axial layout of boulevards, piazzas and monumental centres.

Patrick Usborne proposes the use of 'mat building', arguing that a centre dense enough to reach a critical mass must be built to solve Nanterre's problems. The concept of mat building, outlined by Alison Smithson in 1974, focused on dense flexible frameworks for accommodating growth and change, challenging the separation of architecture and urbanism. Fusing the dense programmatic nature of mat building with the monumentalism of the arcs seen throughout Paris, he proposes a new building type, the MatArc, creating a centre and re-establishing Nanterre Campus as a campus city.

Ensuring MatArc is both a mat building and a monumental arch, the principal process was to convert a planar axial layout to a three-dimensional axial layout. The resulting building contains a radial configuration of 'arc elements' that act to form an arch. The thickness of the boundaries are altered to create programme, resulting in a reverse building type where void is at the centre, the programme surrounds the void and circulation on the periphery. Examples of this happen to be found throughout the Palaces of Paris.

The *voronoi* principal was applied computationally adapting the arc elements, manipulating the ratio between programme and void. The point placement defining each arch element is based on weighted apollonian theory, which increases the control of the size of each arch element and its orientation according to site and programmatic requirements, ensuring a diversity of size. Together, they form a dense mat building where each programme is defined within its arc element with the void at the centre; each programme connected through the arc element as a boulevard, or across to neighbouring programmes.

Nanterre Campus has failed to become the utopian centre it promised to be on the periphery of Paris. MatArc is proposed as a catalyst for a monumental centre, with a critical mass capable of reconfiguring the existing urban fabric to evolve a new centre for growth.

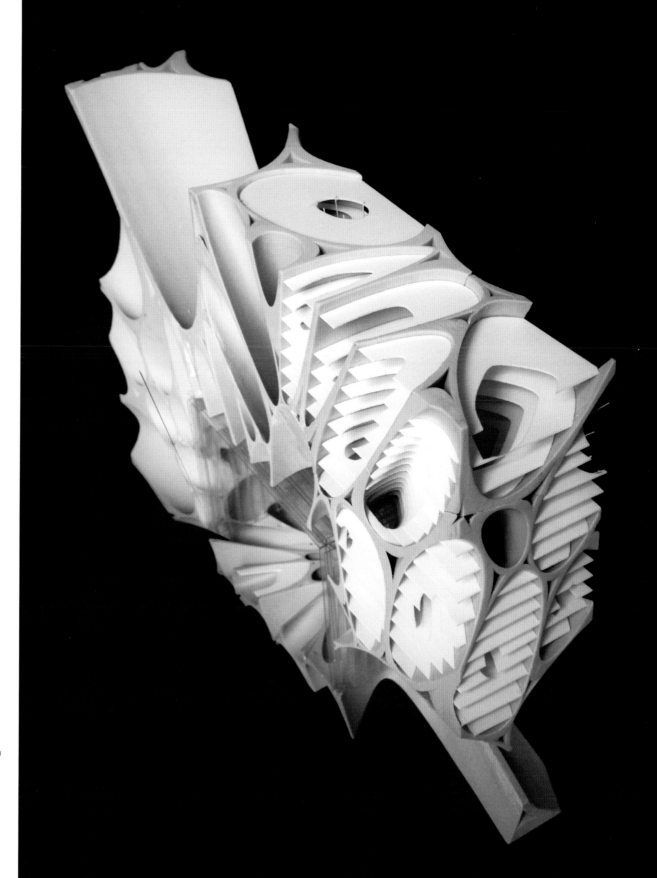

< Plan view of proposal.

> Fragment Model of MatArc.
Scale 1:300. Model dimensions
width 470 height 340 depth
95. Depth of model is 1/5
of actual proposal. The
fragment model emphasises
the three-dimensional axial
configuration that radiates from
a monumental internal void;
forming a *voronoi* packing
of arc elements that creates
a three-dimensional arch; a
MatArc. A monument in itself
that acts as a catalyst for
inevitable reconfiguration of
the surrounding urban fabric.

Alan Dempsey is the founding director of Nex, a multidisciplinary design office with international projects that range in scale from design to architecture and infrastructure. Current work includes two bridges in Dublin, a pavilion with Sir Ken Adam in Berlin and an installation for the furniture manufacturer, Established & Sons, at the Milan Fair.

Alan is a registered architect in the UK and has previously worked with Farjadi Architects, OCEAN and finally with Future Systems, where he was a project director responsible for some of their most significant recent work. Alan studied at the Dublin Institute of Technology, Universidad de los Andes, Bogotá and the Design Research Laboratory (DRL) at the Architectural Association (AA) in London.

Alan was a unit tutor at the AA until 2005, and is currently a co-director of the AA's FAB Research Cluster, which facilitates research projects on novel design and fabrication technologies. He has been an invited critic at universities in the UK and Europe, and his work has been widely published in the US, Europe and Asia, most recently being selected to represent the UK at the 2008 Beijing Architecture Biennale. In 2008, Alan was selected by the British Council as one of the six most significant design entrepreneurs in the UK.

Alvin Huang is a founding director of AL_A, a London-based design studio operating at the intersection of design, technology and materiality. Current work includes a 145,000sqm hotel and shopping complex in Bangkok, Spencer Dock Bridge in Dublin and the Corian Super-surfaces installation in Milan.

Alvin received a Masters of Architecture and Urbanism from the AA's DRL (2004) and a Bachelor of Architecture degree from the University of Southern California (1998). He has worked with DMJM Design, Zaha Hadid Architects and Future Systems. His work has been widely published in the US, Europe and Asia.

He has been an invited critic and guest lecturer at various universities in the UK, Germany, the US and China, and was a tutor in Platform 2: The Next Platform in the School of Interior & Spatial Design at Chelsea College of Art & Design. He is also a founding member of Node (Network of Design Emergence).

[C] SPACE
DRL 10 PAVILION
LONDON & SINGAPORE

This pavilion was the winning entry to an international design competition held by the world renowned Architectural Association school to celebrate the 10th anniversary of their Graduate Design course. The structure was designed for use by the general public and was located on Bedford Square in London, near the British Museum where it provided a rare place for the public to sit and gather informally.

It's visually striking presence invites inspection from a distance and more closely reveals the merging of many discrete flat concrete elements into a single continuous curved form with a thick base that is stepped and ramped to accommodate many different uses.

As you move around, the appearance of the pavilion varies from opaque to transparent, producing a stunning three-dimensional moiré. The 12 metre span structure encloses while also providing a route through for passing pedestrians and blurring the distinction between inside and outside, shelter and stage.

mpetition to celebrate
Association School of
'atory. How does the
achings of the AA,
nce the direction of the

Hooke Parke to the Charles
quare, the AA has a long-
ntal constructions. The (C)
's the result of an open
sign research laboratory
n opportunity to push a
particular, have been
parametric modelling

team of extremely
t the AA with a completed
nature of the project,
most clearly engaged with
the academic discourse of
nterial (Fibre-C) to its limits.

etry is evidently enabled
nputation enter into its

ly, the project was
clusively through digital
e pavilion was modelled
ilised to automate the
structural ribs. Digital
al elements was done
etric modelling tools
etry of the pavilion made
escriptive documents,
KEA flat-pack furniture
dels to facilitate the assembly
e fabricated using waterjet

Q. The project description states that the process developed 16
iterations—what criteria did you use to work towards the final iteration?

A. A number of criteria were used to develop and refine the final result
including:

Structural performance;

Geometric rationalisation;

Joint detailing;

Buildability and construction sequencing; and,

Design intention.

Q. You've used a Sliceform technique to construct the pavilion from
interlocking sets of planar pieces. What are the advantages of this form
of construction?

A. When all the intersections of interlocking elements occur at 90
degree angles, there are a number of advantages to this form of
construction. Unfortunately for us, we didn't have any 90 degree angles!
As such, we had to oversize the notches to get the necessary tolerance
to fit the pieces, and then devise an overlapping and interlocking EPDM
rubber gasket system to lock the joints in place. The original intention
was that this could be done with small flexible rubber gaskets that
would flex into place with no mechanical fixings. Unfortunately, we
weren't able to achieve this.
        Essentially, as the competition was sponsored by the Austrian firm
Rieder CC (manufacturers of a fibre reinforced concrete product called
Fibre-C that comes in pre-fabricated sheets of 3,600mm x 1,200mm
x 13mm), this dictated that the pavilion had to be constructed from
flat panels. This particular assembly technique allowed us to take
advantage of the fact that you can use a series of planar elements
arrayed in a multi-dimensional matrix to produce an assemblage of
complex curvatures.

Q. The design of the pavilion is complex and varied (850+ unique
pieces), but was constructed on a tight budget and a short construction
period. What challenges did you face when going from digital models
into fabrication and construction?

A. Every aspect of this project was challenging! From the structural performance and assembly tolerances to the nomenclature and storage of over 850+ unique panels, the entire project was a real-time learning exercise in managing complexity. Ironically, perhaps the most useful document in the construction and assembly of the entire pavilion was the 1:10 scale laser cut model that was brought out to site as a 3D construction reference. In the end, however, it was a beautiful team effort that made this project possible—the result of many dedicated and hard-working individuals.

Q. How do you see the technological innovations used in the pavilion applied to other projects and how do you see them developing in the future? How have these experiences contributed to your own work?

A. One of the things we are really quick to point out on this project is that there is no such thing as a truly (or solely) digital process. It is really the interface and transfer of technologies and information between the digital and physical that makes things happen. Every parametric process ultimately requires some form of manual refinement. This was a project where we learned immensely from our failures, of which there were many. In this sense, it is truly exciting to see the emergence of 'digital craft', where the dialogue between generative tools, parametric production techniques, manual modelling, material performance / organisation, fabrication and assembly processes become integrated to produce compelling and innovative work, which wouldn't otherwise have been possible. It will be very interesting to see the profession shifting to a point where architects and designers are more in control of the geometries they produce, the dialogues they are facilitating (with consultants, etc) and the procurement process.

TETSURO NAGATA

THE MEMORY THEATRE

In *The Art of Memory* (1966), Frances Yates demonstrates the ancient mnemonic devices that are a means for millennia-enabled orators to remember long speeches and arguments. As Yates explains, in the absence of abundant paper, "the artificial memory was the student's notebook". The *Ars Memoria* utilised virtual spatial organisation of information through the building of memory spaces, which were subsequently navigable. Along the virtual paths, orators would retrieve images to aid the memorising of narratives.

The Middle Ages brought about a transformation in the art of memory. Through the art's reliance on effect, it became increasingly associated with physical representations of striking and unusual human figures, which consequently became a tool of the Church to transfer its teachings to the European populace. And it is this didactic art that one still sees in the paintings and architecture of the mediaeval era. The lasting impression left by *Ars Memoria* on the architecture of western Europe is clear; however the use of its techniques has been largely lost. In an age of digital documentation and playback, Nagata's work revisits these spatial tactics through a series of prototypes leading to his interactive installation, 'Memory Theatre', as detailed below.

The Method Of *Loci*

A small room is populated by commonplace objects that may be used as props for actors to record short video narratives. The library of videos is then projected back onto the objects as uninitiated observers are invited in to explore. A 'difference detection' vision system examines the level of activity within sectors of the installation. When an observer's motion exceeds a specified threshold, the recorded films are triggered and projected back onto the space, revealing fragments of a fictional / non-fictional history.

The Cup Game

Continuing with the use of commonplace objects, this installation is a simple table with a single cup on it. Nagata envisaged the opportunity for each person that moved the cup to be recorded and become part of a history of interventions that are immediately played back projecting down onto the table. The piece subsequently became an investigation into how we continuously remember events in our short-term memory, but rarely make reference to them. With the addition of an overlaid projection, Nagata became interested in how the visualisation of previous manoeuvres built up a reflexive game affecting future decisions at conscious and unconscious levels.

Delay Mirrors

The mirrors take on the personality of a sleepy observer, tired of what it sees. A camera and projection produce a video mirror: the less activity there is in front of it, the more delayed the reflected image becomes, as if forgetting to do its own job. The mirror encourages physical movement as a means of keeping consciousness of real time, and acts as a way in which to self-observe in a manner not possible with a conventional mirror.

Palimpsest Mirror

A literal realisation of the idea of layered wallpaper and the memories stored within them. A projection falls onto an array of transparent sheets where time is manipulated by adding and subtracting the sheets.

Divided into four segments, the observer can construct alternate spatiotemporal reflections through the layering and peeling away of different time states.

Peter Pan's Shadow

Using a computer vision system identifying infrared shadows, a projection displays a 'fake shadow' below people standing within a darkened space. Employing a shadow's innate ambiguity to blur the identities of people, the installation plays with distortions of the truth—toying with the idea of 'false memories' and dreams.

Facial Rose Window

Historically, the rose window is known to express a range of mediaeval ideas of the world, from the importance of geometry and hierarchies to concepts of cycles and the universe. It also uses the implicit nature of order and systems to aid remembering and understanding. Nagata's rose window explored the idea of long-term memory, and a publicly available memory store, by capturing users' faces and projecting them in a calculated array. This reconfigured window can describe a story or a memory. The positioning and distortion of different images form a self-explanatory tale to those who are able to 'read' it.

> The memory theatre as installed at Wates House. From top to bottom: the rose window, delay mirror and dreaming shadow.

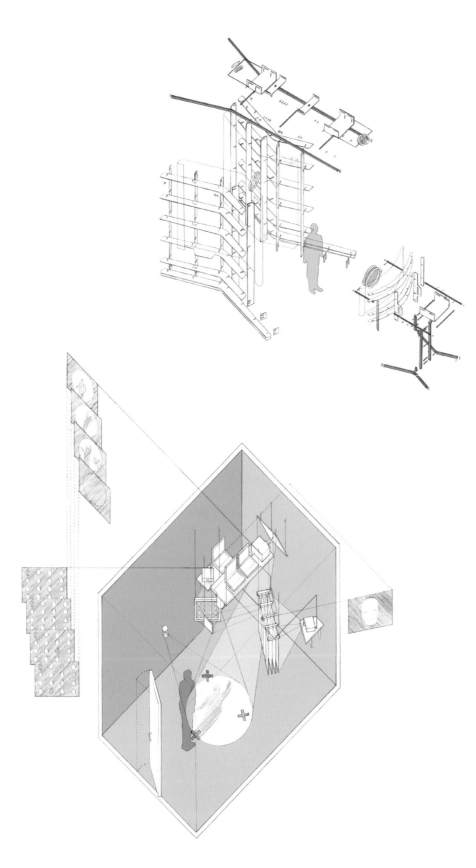

Memory Theatre

To bring coherence to Nagata's series of explorative installations, the work was brought together to explore the networking of memory and the passage between different understandings of memory. This final installation was presented as the 'Memory Theatre' (a reference to Giulio Camillo's Renaissance masterpiece), which uses delayed images of the self to question the observer's own memory. As a processional experience, the installation begins with a spotlight that appears to display an inhabitant shadow on the floor. The shadow begins to delay and then merges into one of a previous inhabitant of the space. The observer is encouraged to approach a delayed mirror in front of them, which, using proximity sensors, shortens its delay the closer they get to it.

At a particular distance, the reflection becomes clearer, and the observer is able to see both their actual and delayed reflection over each other. The piece culminates with the rose window capturing observers' faces and revealing individuals' place in the long-term memory of the space.

When left alone, the installation begins operating without inputs, 'dreaming' or reconstructing its previous memories. The procession evokes that of a church; from nave, to altar and exiting through the west door. Nagata began the project by asking why bodily and facial images have all but disappeared from contemporary architecture, and, as devices that trigger your memory, what their role is in a society obsessed with storing memories in external appliances.

The piece instigates a conversation about image, identity and story telling in a secular world, by questioning the observer's perception of things that are ordinarily taken for granted. Nagata's exploration of the ancient art of memory led him to create an architecture that uses the image of the observer to tell a personal and inquisitive story. Utilising digital technology to instantaneously document events, shorten time and create delays, he uses it to aid in the description of the human memory, in ways that reflect its continual mutability. The meanings and narratives that were set in stone and glass in a bygone era are thereby given a new, dynamic and digital context.

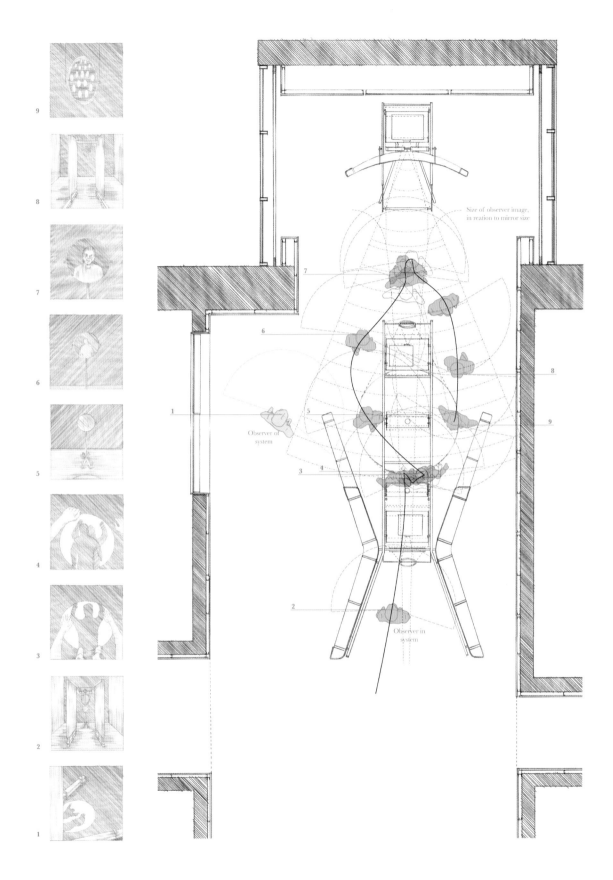

‹^ Manufactured components.

‹⌄ Early iteration combining the
     three 'reflections' of the self.

›   Plan and predicted experience
     of the observer.

TOM DUNN

THE EVOLVING MECHANICAL GARDEN FOR
THE TROPICAL GARDENS OF TRESCO

This project imagines a mechanical garden, constructed as an indigenous architecture, set within the tropical gardens of Tresco in the Scilly Isles facing into the Gulf Stream. This work is born from the premise that to create a truly environmentally sustainable architecture, what is constructed must be part of its surrounding ecosystem.

Early prototyping explored the potential roles for architecture as an ecological catalyst, environmentally adaptive and eventually of Darwinian evolution. This process of making prototypes defined the relationship of digital and analogue fabrication as essential to its construction. Digital techniques were used to survey sites and analogue elements to enable the fabrication of synthetic inserts. The duality of the prototypes' construction demonstrates the need for architecture to combine new digital technology with old analogue techniques to achieve sustainable outcomes. For example, sketches were scanned and used to create CAD drawings to be laser cut, acid etched and then annotated, painted or used for photograms. Prototypes were carved and caste with pewter, formed with CNC cutters and used as components for rotational casting. Through a process of research, testing and prototyping, it became apparent that the final prototype must respond to the fact that all ecosystems are in accelerated flux due to global warming. As a result, my hypothesis was that any genuinely environmentally sustainable architecture must have the ability to evolve to changing climatic conditions.

The tropical gardens site was chosen because it is exposed to the exaggerated effects of global warming and climate change due to facing into the Gulf Stream. The history of man's interaction with his ever-changing environment is recorded in the layers of archaeological data the gardens' roots cling to. While the current climate allows a magnificent tropical garden to exist in the island's unique location, predicted climatic change has the potential to destroy what the locals rely on for their survival. Metrological and environmental data revealed two potential climatic outcomes: a frozen wasteland or a flooded island.

The structures planted within the gardens build up a botanical library in the form of seed banks to enable the garden to survive these two potential outcomes. The process of seed collection is bonded to the structure's mechanical evolution as it responds to a changing climate. To collect the seeds, the outputs of two environmentally adaptive systems that respond to immediate climatic conditions are used.

The systems of collection contain an element of natural selection and also have inbuilt capacities for mutations. The most highly evolved elements of these are combined to create a new system to release the seeds. Thus the architecture constructed goes through one phase of Darwinian evolution to be better suited to its environment.

The first system responds to sunlight levels by melting different waxes with a range of melting temperatures. Seeds are trapped in waxes with a corresponding melting temperature within which they can survive in. A second system responds to moisture levels by eroding at varying rates to release a granite-based sub soil (also trapped with seeds in the wax). The collected seeds are stored and only released when their optimum climatic temperatures reoccur in the future. The proposal constructs a hypothesis by imagining a future environment of extreme flux where qualities of the existing landscape are tended by a flock of 'evolutionary machines', gathering soil, seed and moisture to sustain the gardens' history of alien cultivation.

The project describes a role for architecture and performs an act of preservation for biodiversity in the face of two potentially drastic climatic outcomes. The consequence may be that the work takes on the character of Noah's Ark, a vessel hastily constructed for the gathering of every species, type and form in the face of catastrophe, the only aim being to survive. The other potential is that the seeds are stored in insulated capsules within a frozen landscape waiting for suitable climatic conditions to reoccur, triggering their release. The battle for survival of the architecture, and the gardens it relies on, are recorded in the layers of soil that build up around the structure, rooting it to its harsh environment in an archaeological record of architectural interaction for future generations to read.

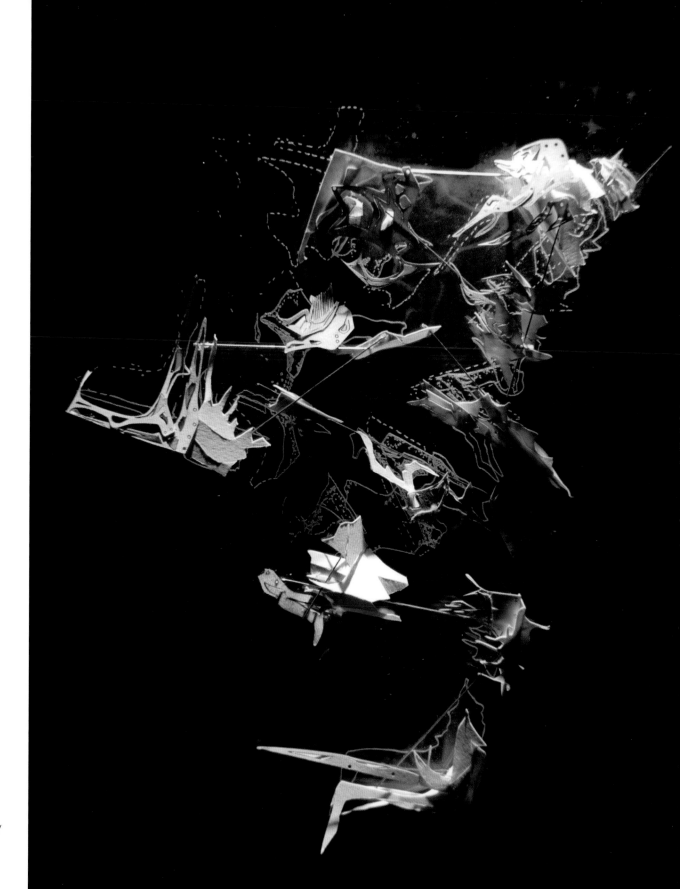

> Maquettes of Environmentally
Adaptive System.

> Evolving Mechanical Garden
> for Tresco: Final Prototype 1:10.

˅ Environmental Control:
Water Overflow System.

˅˃ Environmental Control:
Water Overflow System.

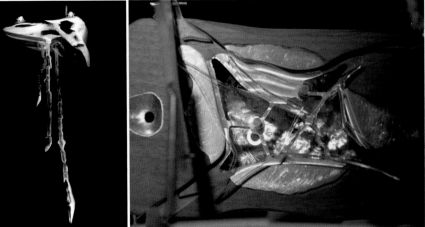

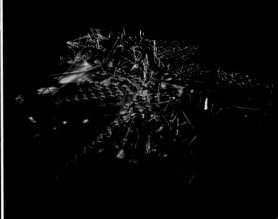

MARILENA SKAVARA

ADAPTIVE FA[CA]DE

Today's technology places architects on the threshold of a new era of 'intelligent' kinetic architecture. Kinetic façade systems in the built environment are increasingly popular for solar shading, but the performative opportunities of these systems are largely unexamined. The few exceptions would include dECOi's Hyposurface, Slow Furl by Mette Ramsgard Thomsen and Karin Bech, Flare by WHITEvoid and Ruairi Glynn's Reciprocal Space.

Marilena Skavara's 'Adaptive Fa(ca)de' explores the functional possibilities and performative characteristics of cellular automata (CA). In addition to the unique emergent behaviour of CA, a neural network enables a further computational layer to evolve CA behaviour to the context of its surrounding environment. Building upon the early work of Conway's 'Game of life' and Stephen Wolfram's extensive research on the wider implementation of CA, Skavara's facade becomes a living adapting skin, constantly training itself from the history of its own errors and achievements.

CA Patterns

CA are defined as a finite grid of cells where time is discrete and each cell inherits its state depending on the state of its neighbours and itself in the previous instance. The declaration of the neighbourhood land rule is crucial for this emergent system. The simplest CA configurations are binary, but more discrete states can be applied on the cells. In the case of Skavara's facade, a totalistic CA is chosen with a neighbourhood consisting of three cells and seven states, correlating to a respective number of tilting angles.

The Seven States, Neighbourhood of Three Cells

To generate CA patterns with the goal of optimising the light levels to a building interior, a multilayer artificial neural network is trained. Following numerous training iterations to create a self-regulating system, the façade is tested against 'novel data'. To evaluate its success, a virtual model is created making a number of presumptions regarding orientation, materiality and optimum light intensity.

Attempting to solve functional goals by relinquishing partial control of the building to evolve its own strategies is in marked contrast to the typically predeterminate behaviour of contemporary solar shading systems. Exploring the critical balance of complexity and order, Skavara produces a continually novel choreography offering methods of evolutionary digital design that lead to playful, adaptive and performative architecture.

˅ Robotic facade fragment, 25 Servo Driven panels mounted on Perspex and SLS 3D printed frame.

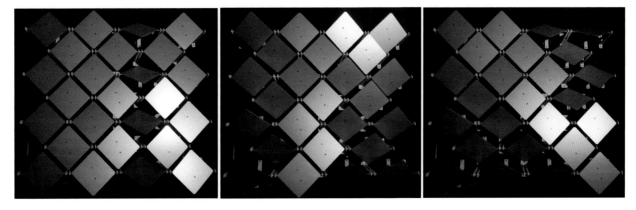

LABYRINTHS MAZES & SPACES INBETWEEN

SAM MCELHINNEY

Among the myriad of architectural devices inherited from the ancient and classical worlds, the concept of the labyrinth and its counterpoint, the maze, are often overlooked in our field of study. Despite offering both an archetypal architect (Deadalus) and artifice (the Minoan legend), the field of labyrinth study is rarely deeply engaged with in theoretical terms; beyond the excellent taxonomic work of Ben Nicholson, the explicit development of this rich conceptual subject in contemporary architectural thinking is rare.

It is impossible (and unnecessary) to fully describe the many threads of labyrinthine understandings here. Conceptually, however, it is highly concerned with immediate, individual, bodily space and the formation and occupancy of it. It is also important to note the often missed distinction between the labyrinth and the maze: the former a single, (monocursal) folding path that if faithfully followed will ultimately reach its destination; the latter contains multiple paths, branches and dead ends, specifically designed to confuse the occupant.

Within the field of architecture, one regularly adopts a hypothetical modelling approach in order to test out a particular design; fundamental to which is the assumption that the observer / occupier of the work has particular values. In aggregating a series of these assumptions, architects knowingly or unknowingly create an internal model of the user, often based upon their own likes or dislikes.

One area in which the explicit fashioning of a 'construct' of the user has provided some involved debate is in the research of movement; why and how we make decisions during our occupancy of spaces and the greater or lesser extent to which these can be seen as predictable. Having become fascinated by this field, it occurred to me that this discussion could be well re-informed with an understanding of the interrelation between the polar typologies of labyrinth and maze.

'cretan' type labyrinth drawn on an isometric grid.

The Two Users

The labyrinth-user accepts and internalises a route that has been presented in symbol form. By following this, they are free to engage in abstract, introvert and reflective thought. Given a predetermined external bodily path, the labyrinth walker seeks out cogent internal mental paths. This observed occupant, despite apparently being wholly predictable (walking a set path), is more likely to develop novel internal thoughts or solutions. This may be expressed through an abrupt, unanticipated change of behaviour, direction or even departure from the labyrinth's 'thinking-space'.

Conversely, a maze-user is not provided with a solution; they have to attempt to 'find their way', doing so by engaging in a direct dialogue with their surroundings. An immediate, continual assessment of novelty within the environment primes simple mechanisms in a decision-making process; a response to experienced stimuli or pre-learnt social constructs. In this way, 'dead ends' might be spotted or apparently longer routes favoured. The commonality of these responses means that movement can be predicted.

Over time, successful movements might assemble to form a coherent enough understanding for the environment to be reconsidered as containing a 'labyrinth' solution. Prior to this, internal reasoning is of little benefit to a system operating in real-time in the real world 'maze'.

Beyond

It seems reasonable to extrapolate this model of two users. Indeed, architecture could be considered wholly in terms of labyrinths or mazes, and our maze- and labyrinth-user constructs could refer to more general occupant movements and spatial understandings. This classification is not a simple division. More often than not the understandings are coincident, overlapping and fluctuating as the environment and the user's comprehension change. Novel, unexplored spaces and active architectures can be considered initially maze-like. Their observers or occupants gather delight in the same way, through gradually constructing their understanding. This does not preclude labyrinthine thought; architecture tends to be formed from identifiable components such as arcades or stairways and these familiarities are augmented by learnt social constructs. Recognition of these patterns prompts moments of reflective thought.

Places where deep introspection and reflection occur tend to be highly personal and intimately known or constructed in isolation from real-world activity. These labyrinthine spaces include religious buildings or private gardens. Within these, prompts are found that help create 'novel constancy'; for example, rhythmic choral chants, even the repetitive movement of digging.

As a space becomes learnt, its labyrinthine aspect emerges. The high activity of most real-world environments means that an element of maze is almost always present, explaining why we are often predictable; the noise of continually changing stimuli through which we walk causing reversion to maze-navigation behaviour.

My premise is that all space is found, experienced and inhabited in a state of 'switching' flux between the diametrically opposed typologies of maze and labyrinth, offering insights into the evocation of a continual delight in the architectural user. It could be argued that we fashion spaces that aid mediation between these forms of movement and spatial comprehension. Perhaps we constantly seek to move from one to the other, seeking novelty and delight in our methods of understanding. In navigating our built environment, we perceive different spatialities by continually switching from movement in a maze-like mode to a labyrinthine one and back—a flowing process not yet explored in architectural research.

Between

I am primarily concerned with what it means for users to engage a path that switches from a labyrinth into a maze (or vice-versa). Diagrammatically this switch is not between, but from labyrinth path to anti-path (commonly illustrated as the 'wall'); topologically fully or partially collapsing the labyrinth and creating maze situations.

This poses many questions: How might it be constructed? What are the experiential ramifications of inhabiting it? What might we learn from observing its occupants? Repeated visits to such an environment might enable it to learn about its occupants; interaction between the two might form recognisable emergent architectural elements and movements showing attempted labyrinth formulation.

From this position, I began two new lines of experimentation; both attempting to explore the bi-polar user construct.

A maze-agent ecology
Dialogues

Using processing, an in-silico experimental environment was set up consisting of a series of 'doors' set out on a triangular grid forming a 'maze matrix'. Each door was capable of being closed, primed or open. A simple cascade algorithm could induce the doors to open in sequence, enabling the maze to create coherent stable routes through itself. As these routes wrap around onto themselves, a series of spaces are created; some 'room like', others 'corridors'.

The matrix has an innate goal—desiring to exist in a 'resolved' state, with coherent path structures. It remains like this until disturbed by the new opening of a door, at which point the cascade restarts.

A series of simple agents were designed based on the principles of active perception, each 'looking' along a series of 'depth vectors' at a resolution time approximate to our sight. Their real time self-resolution of surrounding 'visual depths' offers potential development in this field of work. On being introduced to the maze, the agents were given the capability to open doors at will, triggering a reconfiguration of the stable routes. Each agent also had a series of desires compelling it to seek out or attempt to construct particular 'spatialities', either 'rooms' or 'corridors'. After a period of time spent either successfully occupying or unsuccessfully searching for a particular spatiality, the agent became bored or frustrated and changed its goals respectively. This led to a complex emergent series of dialogues between the desires of the agents (to explore or to accept the current configuration) and their environment (attempting to resolve into coherent routes), which can be read in the trails of the agents.

Individual agent exploration paths through the reconfiguring maze were recorded as overlaid Muybridge-type images. Careful study allowed categorisation into distinct movement typologies:

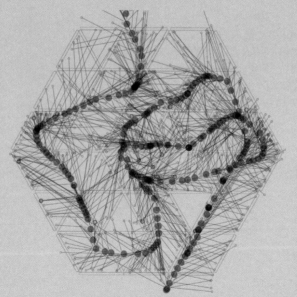

Trans-type—from sustained and direct path seeking and following;

Interrupted trans-type—from periods of path seeking and following punctuated with one or two phases of sustained room seeking and occupancy;

Return type—periods of path seeking and following interspersed with shorter phases of room seeking and occupancy;

Meander—room seeking and occupancy desires outweigh those of path seeking. A turning, 'exploratory' path evolves;

Orbital—the two systems' desire sets are equally weighted; and,

Complex knot—allowing a continual variation of desire priorities results in hybrid combinations and linkages of the path types.

Each different movement typology appears to be directly related to a specific modulation of the desires of individual agents; expressing these outwardly as distinctive dance patterns that attempt to achieve spatial goals. Lacking the ability for internal thought, the agents are engaging an external 'bodily' reasoning process in their attempts to manipulate and navigate the maze.

Some of the agents' movements seem directly equitable to forms that have been long since established as successful elements of labyrinth construction; the meander and orbit clearly show some form of relationship here. This is particularly intriguing, suggesting that the structure of a labyrinth might emergently form from within a maze as it accommodates patterns of human exploratory desire, intimately linking the wanderings of the mind, the abilities of the body and the path of the labyrinth.

Emergence

A spin off was devised exploring the idea of emergence within the maze matrix. Each door was given the ability to 'observe' and record agent proximities, counting the number of times it is directly opened and keeping a 'heat' count that increments up whenever an agent actually passes through.

Data from the doors was used in various algorithms to control which door was opened next in the resolving cascades. The simplest was a random number generator—later ones chose the door that had been opened the most times by an agent, walked through the most or walked through the least. Giving the maze the ability to refuse to open a door to an agent (or immediately shut it again) allowed two more algorithms that made 'less walked through' doors harder to open and 'most walked through' doors hard to open.

By depicting doors that were closed for 70%+ of the total experiment run-time, a pattern was recorded that illustrated which doors approximated to walls. A second recording marked each agent's route as a spline trail. Over 30 agent-visits emergent 'tracks' (common agent paths) and 'screens' (structures formed from closed doors) could be seen.

When the maze is passive (not re-resolving routes in a cascade manner), the agents gradually independently opened routes through: if pre-opened a route remained dominant until 'boredom' movements by the agents broke it down.

Once the maze was set to actively re-configure upon a door being opened, altering the maze control algorithms profoundly affected how it achieved its goal state. This influenced movement over a series of agent 'visits'.

Using a random door choice algorithm to open the next door in the cascade produced an average configuration of concentric rings of 'screens', rather like a courtyard and cloister. Agent 'exploration urges' were expressed by crossing between the rings. This configuration reoccurred repeatedly with later algorithms, forming a first generational phase before dissolving into more specific and complex structures.

The more observational algorithms gave two clear results: those that sought to predict and 'satisfy' agent door choice caused diagonal screen structures to emerge, promoting access deep into the matrix; and, those that sought to predict and 'frustrate' agent movement produced markedly different screen formations—lateral, rather than diagonal structures formed, preventing forward movement and forcing agents to explore sideways. High densities of movement near the maze entrance meant that this was particularly marked here; an emergent vestibule space arose. In later generations, the lateral screens behind this dissolved into single panels creating a central area of engagement and free exploration.

Each ecology involved a series of clear generational phases. Given that each depicts a fragment of reasoning between the maze and the agents, their accumulation over time forms the construction of an accord between the two systems; the maze in particular develops an understanding of how it is being understood. This 'learning' is expressed in the 'screen' constructions—the maze becomes increasingly effective at influencing inhabitation to suit its desires.

The results are neo-architectures that hint at roots of architectural elements, emerging from and to control inhabitation. These morphologies are the results of a dialogue that endeavours to develop coherence. We began with a maze and have shown that even the simplest systems can demonstrate abilities to mould spatiality into labyrinthine (or understood) architectures.

A switching labyrinth
Developed as part of a theoretical work exploring the nature of our knowing and inhabitation of novel space for Bartlett School of Architecture's end of year show (June 2009), it provided a framework for a further two months of experimental occupation and observation.

This full scale built installation consisted of approximately 250 metres of black fabric curtains hung from a suspended space-frame, forming a series of pathways that wrapped around two small 'room' spaces. Each 'room' contained four sliding curtain 'doors', individually animated by a stepper motor and slide mechanism, which were able to periodically shift, so 'switching' openings to offer alternative entrance and exit routes.

As different doors were opened and closed, different combinations of labyrinthine path were linked. Each 'door' was given an innate memory of their shifting position within the matrix relative both to one another and to the overall path arrangement. By employing a processing algorithm similar to that used by the previous 'in silico' mazes, the doors were able to work in dialogue together to construct complete, coherent and stable labyrinth routes within the installation. Inhabitants were observed by the installation using an array of 56 pressure pads and their movement became another influence upon the path resolution process. While occupants followed the path, the installation configuration remained stable, but as they deviated the sliding curtains began to selectively move in reaction. This process collapsed the current labyrinth structure and produced periods of fragmentary 'maze-like' path arrangements.

As the occupant and installation respectively 'learnt' about one another's expected behaviour patterns, negotiated labyrinth routes were found to gradually evolve and key typologies repeatedly became dominant. Following on from the agent-based work, it suggests an explorative desire basis for the emergence of labyrinthine, or familiar, spatialities within an unknown or changing maze framework. This is a process of entanglement, with the bodily space of occupant movements gradually wrapping around each other over time and leaving accretions that form architecture.

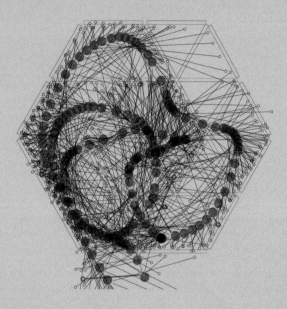

‹ ^ 'complex knot' type trails showing movement of a 'vector vision' agent in an observing and reacting maze matrix.

MATTHEW SHAW

SUBVERTING THE LIDAR LANDSCAPE: TACTICS OF SPATIAL REDEFINITION FOR A DIGITALLY EMPOWERED POPULATION

Exploring the difference between virtual freedoms and physical constraints imposed by the urban environment, this project proposes urban alterations within a city centre that afford physical freedoms akin to those experienced digitally.

Digital Sight

The virtual environment is home to a multitude of representations of the physical world, varying from factual reference sources to make-believe fantasy worlds. Google Earth, for example, is a popular method of urban spatial research and often taken as virtual fact. This is a representation of urban data collected *via* modern surveying techniques, including landscape scale 3D-scanning or LiDAR. This data forms part of a growing spatial data-bank increasingly available to designers and an interactive public.

The 'open source movement' is not only hosting much of this spatial data, but can provide tools for its collection. This project uses DavidScanner, an open-source 3D-scanning software that enables amateurs to build and operate a desktop 3D scanner from readily available materials that can achieve the quality of an industry standard scanner.

With these tools in mind, this project proposes a greater interaction between peoples' digital spatial ambitions (currently vast) and the way that they inhabit their urban environments (comparatively limited). Understanding of virtual and global space lies well beyond the limits of peoples' physical grasp, and this project aims to provide tools for urban environments to not only reflect this freedom but encourage and facilitate it.

Spatial Subversion

This project deals with the potential to edit digital versions of physical space and the possible misalignment of the virtual and the real. A series of tools and interventions act to subvert these facts at their point of data collection, rather than through editing the data itself. These become tools for spatial redefinition and a medium for publishing truths, mistruths, etc. These subversions do not exist in a purely virtual world, although this is where they are most effectual, instead they are often physical objects / additions / alterations to the urban fabric. These interfere

with the collection of virtual data, but also act as facts on the ground and waypoints linking a physical and virtual world. When urban surveying techniques come into contact with these objects, they offset, demolish, etc, their understanding of the urban landscape around them.

Some examples:

The 'stealth drill' for boundary dissolution and private seeping: Used to create new urban routes, views and spaces, and also allow the spilling and leaking of different spatial properties;

The gap location device and mobile loophole detection unit: Mobile LiDAR units that survey the urban environment looking for confusing and misleading spatial data;

Boundary miscommunication devices forming the public redecoration zone: Insurgent interventions that publish, record and broadcast new spatial truths and mistruths;

Insurgent gateway: Forms a hollow patch in the LiDAR data, a point of no information, occurring either through purposeful deletion of virtual data or an intentionally LiDAR repelling physical object that deflects data to a perimeter distance; and,

The flash architecture unit: A rapidly assembled piece of stealth architecture projecting a much vaster version of itself when scanned.

Amalgamated Fabrication

The project has evolved both its material and formal language through a process of digital-made and analogue-made experimentations that create the objects above. They proceeded more as making discussions and tests than the simple building of pre-designed objects. In its development, each object passes through a series of physical and digital prototypes, together creating a final object, each stage providing new insight into the relationship between a physical object and its digital counterpart.

While the project at large deals with landscape scale 3D-scanning, each object is made using the same technology but on a desktop scale, its design constantly tested and redefined by its technologies.

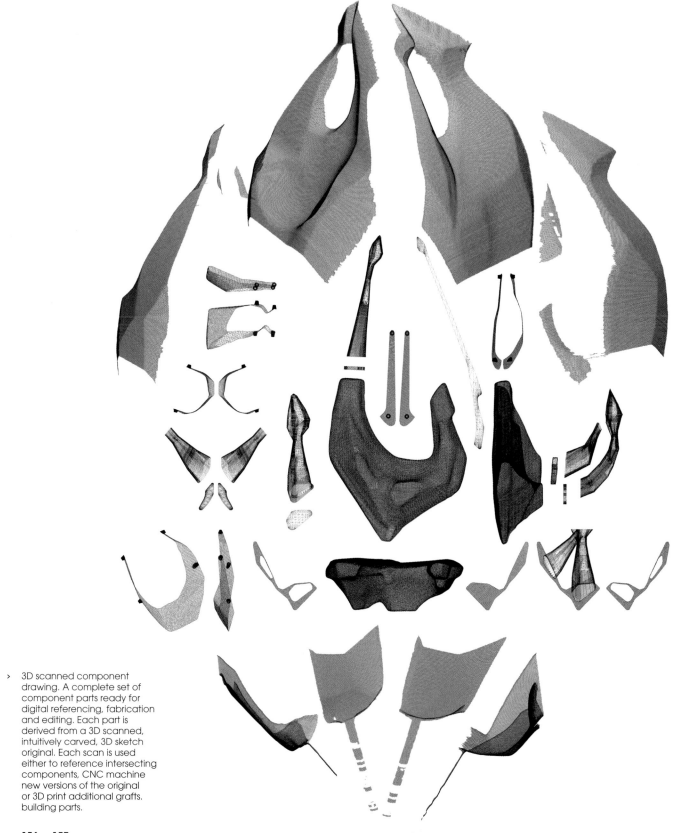

> 3D scanned component
drawing. A complete set of
component parts ready for
digital referencing, fabrication
and editing. Each part is
derived from a 3D scanned,
intuitively carved, 3D sketch
original. Each scan is used
either to reference intersecting
components, CNC machine
new versions of the original
or 3D print additional grafts.
building parts.

The Process

Intuitive hand-carved 3D pieces become three-dimensional sketchbooks for positioning the next set of components to be added. Tagged and referenced with annotations to guide their manipulation once brought into a digital realm, they are then 3D-scanned using a developed version of the open source 3D-scanning software. Images can be mapped onto the surface of each scan so that sketches and annotations from the physical objects can be transferred to the digital. The reference points drawn earlier allow individual scans to be digitally aligned to compile a complete digital version of the object.

CAD-designed components, jigs and grafts are created to fit the original object exactly, and then 3D-printed using SLS technology. Digitally-altered versions of the objects are then used to create replica pieces in a new material using CNC machinery. The accurate 3D scan of the object surface also allows CNC precision alterations and interventions to the original object itself.

Silicone moulds are then made (using traditional mould-making technique) from the original carved objects with their digitally-created additional components and used to cast CNC components within a new clear silicone of the original carved objects.

To gain the palette of materials and finish techniques from which the final objects are manufactured, a 3D scanner is used throughout to test the accuracy of made components and the ambiguity and confusion created by different forms, materials and surface finishes. Black gloss finishes and transparent objects were two of the most successful subversive material combinations, which led to to the use of machined black acetal plastic and transparent casting silicone in the final pieces.

This material and formal language of stealth and confusion was developed through scanning to achieve invisibility, inaccuracy and abstraction, resulting in a design process with an emphasis on stealth mechanics and on making the unscanable.

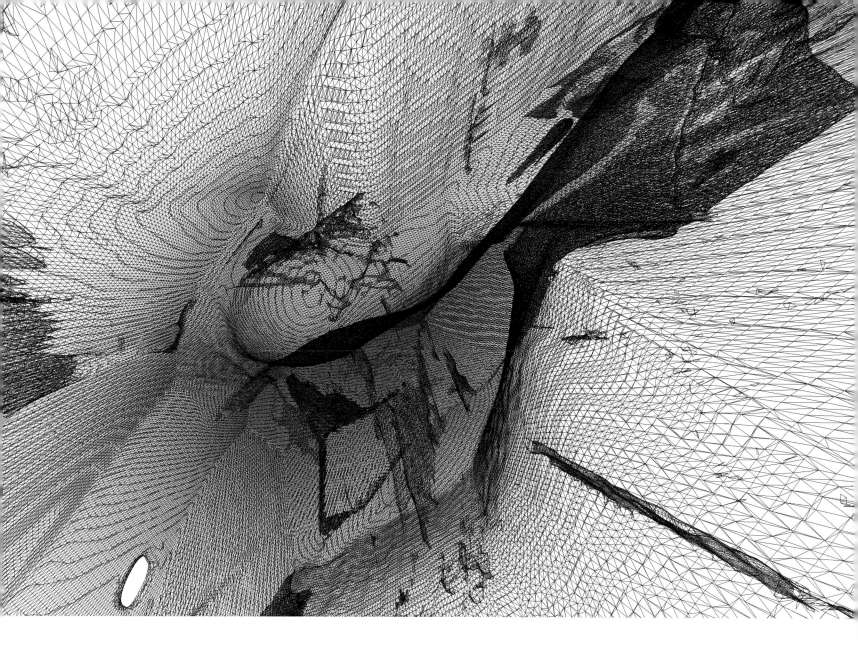

‹ Hand carved original objects.

∧ Subverting the LiDAR Landscape in Parliament's zone of ambiguity. A perspective aerial scan of Westminster showing the effects of strategically deployed stealth tools. Show here is the public redecoration zone, an urban transplant and graft, a series of stealthdrill toolpaths, a LiDAR shield, the insurgent gateway and the Huas-MattaClarkian vista.

The term 'plasma' as the 'fourth state of matter' indicates a receptive and responsive design process—a 'formation' through the coordination of forces and the involvement of dynamic parameters.

The studio is working on all scales, from furniture and installations to urbanism and master planning. Starting with a range of small but challenging refurbishment projects in London between 1999 and 2002, Plasma then completed various new buildings in the Italian Dolomites, where it opened a branch with partner Ulla Hell in 2002. Combining complex geometries with local materials, the studio seeks to develop a new local vernacular inspired by the landscape instead of the traditional building typology.

Between 2003 and 2005, Plasma worked alongside some of the most famous architects on one of the floors of Hotel Puerta America, Madrid. Plasma's floor was one of the most challenging of the 16 radically different takes and was widely published. This brought the practice international attention.

Recently, Plasma has been involved in large-scale mixed-use projects in China, and is currently lead designer for the International Horticultural Expo in Xi'an, with 37ha and 12,000m^2 of projected buildings. The project, which opens in 2011 to approximately 200,000 visitors a day, enables Plasma to develop a complete and integrated sustainable vision.

Plasma won the BD/Corus Young Architect of the Year Award and the Hot Dip Galvanising Award in 2002, the Next Generation Architects Award in 2007 and the Contract World Award in 2008. Additionally, Plasma was selected for *Architecture Record*'s Design Vanguard 2004 and *Arquitectura Viva's Emergentes* in 2007. Its work has been widely published, for example: Phaidon's *10x10_2* and *Atlas of 21st Century Architecture*, Taschen's *Architecture Now*, the *Architectural Review*, *A+U*, *Abitare*, *Architektur Aktuell*, *Icon*, *Mark*, *Wallpaper**, the *New York Times*, the *Financial Times* and *El Pais*, among many others.

Plasma Studio has had many international exhibitions and often developed a specific installation for each, most importantly: Solo exhibition at Suitcasearchitecture Gallery, Berlin 2002; The Crumple Zone at Emerson Studios, London 2003; Fluxo Rosa at the Instituto Cultural de Michoacan, Morelia, Mexico 2004; Transpositional Practice—solo exhibition at the Architectural Association, London 2005; 3G—inaugural installation at 'Extension gallery', Chicago 2006; and, solo exhibition at Galleria di Architettura '*come se*', Rome.

PLA
ST

FLOWING GARDENS XI'AN INTERNATIONAL HORTICULTURAL EXPO 2011

An international competition winner Flowing Gardens creates a consonant functionality of water, planting, circulation and architecture into one seamless system.

The landscape is organised by a tessellated network of paths. At the major intersections of these three buildings have been developed as intensification of the ground condition.

The Gate building operates on the level of infrastructure and fulfills the role of bridging over the main road that dissects the site. It therefore channels the visitors from the entry plaza, where they congregate and orient themselves after having entered into the expo and sets them into a definite direction.

Above a weaving undulating land bridge that provides compelling views of the whole landscape ahead, we employ an innovative tensegrity structure forming a trellis to become overgrown by greenery.

The Exhibition building is located on the edge of the lake as the endpoint to the central axis as well as the starting point for the crossing of the water by boat. It ties in with the series of piers that read as the landscape jetting out into the water.

On the other side of the lake, the Greenhouse will be the third and last major building to be visited and is shaped as a precious crystal semi-submerged in splendid isolation. Visitors transgress along a tessellated mesh of paths through three different climatic zones with the corresponding plant environments.

Interview with Holger Kehne

Q. The studio received the Next Generation Architects/Pipers Award in 2008 and the Young Architect of the Year Award in 2002. You have been successfully developing your own signature style through small projects—how would you describe this and how has it changed with the more recent larger international projects, such as the Flowering Garden project in Xi'an, China?

A. We worked for the first three years on tiny refurbishment projects in London, gradually extending our scope and scale. In 2003, we received the commission for the Hotel Puerta America and also started a range of new-built projects in Northern Italy, for example the Strata Hotel. From the start we consistently worked on competitions that addressed the larger scale. In this way, we developed our work as essentially 'scaleless'.

The same geometric principle may apply to both the urban layout or to a detail of the same project. The Xi'an International Horticultural Fair has enabled us to apply this style for the first time. The 37ha of landscape has been organised as a branching pattern of paths, and the buildings become a finer grain of the same logic that then become structures and even furniture.

Q. How do you go about developing your projects and where do you seek inspiration?

Inspiration usually develops from within the process itself. We extract a certain logic that then develops into form and material.

Q. Your work is clearly enabled by digital processes evident in your interests in complex geometry. At what stage do computers enter into the design process?

A. With us, there is no particular moment that the computer enters into the process. We may actually start on the computer and then later move to develop using hand-sketched diagrams or physical models. The computer helps to facilitate the transfer of material and ideas between different modes of enquiry, and supports our process-based approach.

Q. What is your favourite project of the studio to date and why? Could you tell us a little about the process behind this project?

Our favourite project to date is Hotel Puerta America. It was instrumental in pursuing and developing our vision without compromise and down to the smallest detail. It has an intensity that still blows us away each time we visit—how on earth did they let us do this?

The first thing that the clients said was: "We don't want to interfere with your creativity". So they didn't give us a brief; and it took a while before we could operate and fully enjoy that unconstrained artistic freedom. But eventually we really grasped it as a unique opportunity and pushed the project to its limits.

Q. What work by other young artist / designers / architects do you find interesting?

A. There are plenty of interesting young architects and designers all around the world that seem to share similar concerns. But we are still more inspired by artists, because their approach is slightly different, more unbound. For example, the Weather project by Olafur Eliasson used very simple material moves to completely change Tate Modern's Turbine Hall from a vacuous space into a mystical, 'outworldly' event. Another favourite is Ernesto Neto, who explores the relationship between form and material much more freely and evocatively than most architects are able to do.

Q. You run a studio at the Architectural Association (AA), which in recent years has led parametricism as a technique for architectural design. Where does your studio agenda fit into the AA's direction? Is this studio a platform to find opportunities to develop techniques for your own practice?

A. The studio and AA Diploma Unit 12 are cross-fertilising each other. Neither is more experimental than the other—but there are differences. With Plasma, we have less time to develop the initial concept, but then a lot more time to refine it. We also consciously build on existing projects, so we don't start from scratch with each new work. The students, on the other hand, bring in their own unique personalities and previous experiences, so there is a wider gamut of possibilities.

Q. How important is it for you to keep up-to-date with new developments in digital design and fabrication?

A. Parametric tools and a three-dimensional building model are routine now. This shapes the design process and allows for a wider scope as changes can be implemented further down the line than previously possible. A project like Xi'an, with its changing goalposts, would have been very difficult to execute without digital design tools. Similarly, a lot of our built work relies on digital fabrication to make complex geometries feasible.

Q. What advice would you offer young graduates today?

A. It's a difficult time now, in stark contrast to previous years. When we finished in the 1990s, however, we were faced with a similar picture. We couldn't find the right jobs, so we started off on our own with tiny jobs that nevertheless became really formative. However, five years were spent working below the breadline, so an alternative may be to go abroad and gain experience where there is work, such as in China.

Q. What's next for your practice and the industry as a whole?

A. We hope we can continue to develop our vision to integrate architecture, landscape and infrastructure in a wide variety of new projects globally.

Besides Xi'an, we are currently working on two industrial buildings in Italy, a holiday house in Uganda, a sculpture for a tower in Dubai, the design of street lamps for an Italian company and an invited competition for a theatre extension.

We trust that the more inventive and serious architects will adapt to the current challenges. Hopefully, they will be able to strengthen their position in order to foster a real—and currently very necessary—change.

Time, Performance, Kinetics

Although Vitruvius's treaties included clocks, waterworks and mobile war machines, architecture is often understood to be an art of space, not time. Architecture's traditional role has been the spatial backdrop to social interaction: In the 20th Century, Archigram's 'Instant City', Negroponte's 'Soft Architecture Machines', Price's 'Fun Palace' and 'Generator' projects challenged this axiom, imagining and constructing architectures that were interactive participants in their own right.

While these architectures borrowed much from the mechanical automata, kinetic sculpture and early cybernetic arts, they imagined more than simple choreographed kinetics routines. They suggested an architecture able to propose and negotiate its own kinetic behaviour with the world around it, one that could enter into a conversation (or even perhaps a dance) with its inhabitants. Often, however, these visions of interactive architectures were limited to the drawing board by the technical possibilities of the time. Today's technology places architects on the threshold of a new era of 'intelligent' kinetic architecture.

Artists, architects and designers are increasing investigating the creative uses of low cost sensing, computation and actuating technologies. With huge growth in open source initiatives and online communities, once difficult financial and knowledge base obstacles have been considerably diminished. "The 21st Century designer will have to be fluent in automatic, reactive and interactive design, i.e. Time based design in its three forms. Designers and architects are faced with an essentially new extension to their craft." (Gage 2002)

To understand and develop this craft, one must first identify these three forms of time-based design. If we consider 'automatic' design, to be the creation of such artefacts as clocks, repeating kinetic sculptures and cinematic film, then 'reactive' design differs from these automata, in that reactive artefacts have some ability to be triggered by stimuli that causes a change in their output. Examples include anything from simple bedside lamps, building elevators and home security systems to mp3 players, digital cameras and touch screen kiosks.

All of these reactive systems, whether elements of our built environment, artworks or consumer gadgets, have (to varying levels of complexity) a range of preset content/behaviours that can be triggered to change.

Interactive architecture

How, then, does the third form of time-based design, 'interactive' differ from 'reactive' design? It's a question that surprisingly stops most so-called 'interaction designers' in their tracks. Perhaps one explanation for this lack of distinction is, as Glanville calls it, "terminological inflation". 'Interactivity' has become a buzzword used to encompass many technologies that provide some form of 'reaction' to a 'user' input. "They perform tricks, but they do not give us anything that is remotely interactive, nor is there any meaningful sharing: simply a response to some stimulus in an action/reaction mode." (Glanville, 2001)

As a result, the widespread misuse of the term 'interactivity', has trivialised its meaning to the point that it holds no more conceptual value than 'reactivity' to most of today's artists, architects and designers.

I believe the common use of the term 'interactivity', particularly in so-called human computer interaction design, is flawed. Most interaction design today is an aesthetic enhancement of models of reactive design rooted in the earliest methods of computer instruction; a rigid and restrictive master/slave model. I argue that a more useful and productive model for interactivity is dialogue or conversation, naturally occurring between human beings and in the wider animal kingdom. Other architects exploring this model include Usman Haque, Adam Somlai Fischer, Michael Fox, Mark Shepard, Omar Khan, Stephen Gage and Ranulph Glanville.

Using this understanding of interactivity as a conversational exchange between participants, I will briefly present what I consider to be, the current (mis)use of the term interactivity in artistic discourse, examining celebrated examples of so-called 'interactive' art works. I will then go on to develop this argument by presenting my 'Performative Ecologies'—a series of interactive environments that explore and demonstrate the conceptual distinctions I have made. This will focus on the most recent iteration presented at the Digital Hinterlands and Tent Digital Exhibitions in 2009.

The installation is made up of a community of conversational objects called 'dancers' that engage with people and other dancers in an evolving performance.

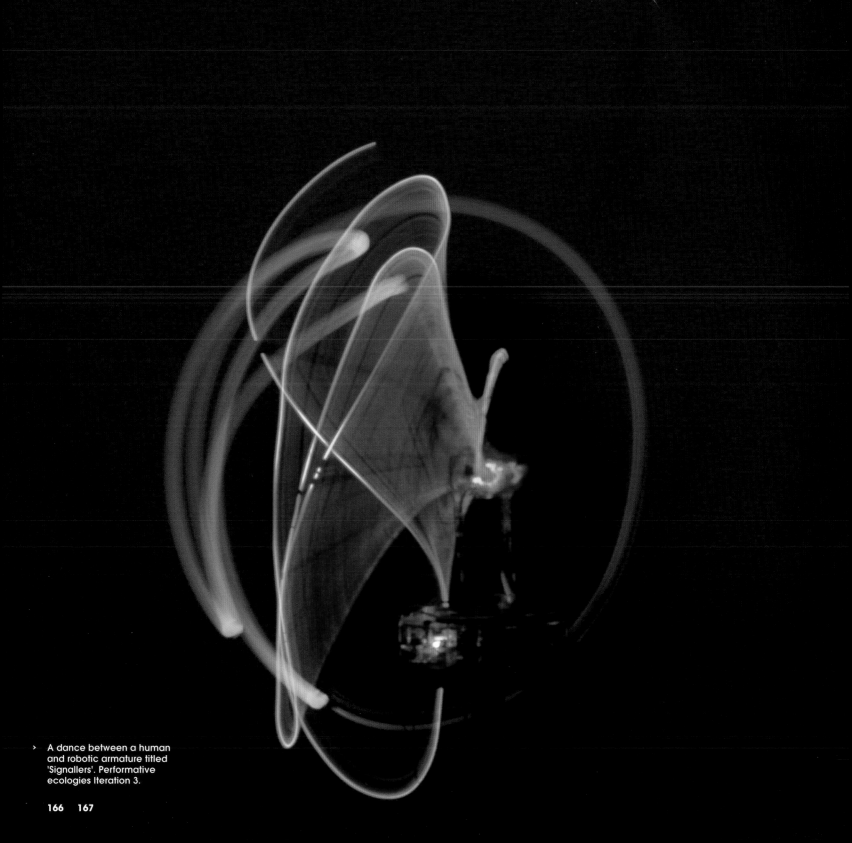

> A dance between a human and robotic armature titled 'Signallers'. Performative ecologies Iteration 3.

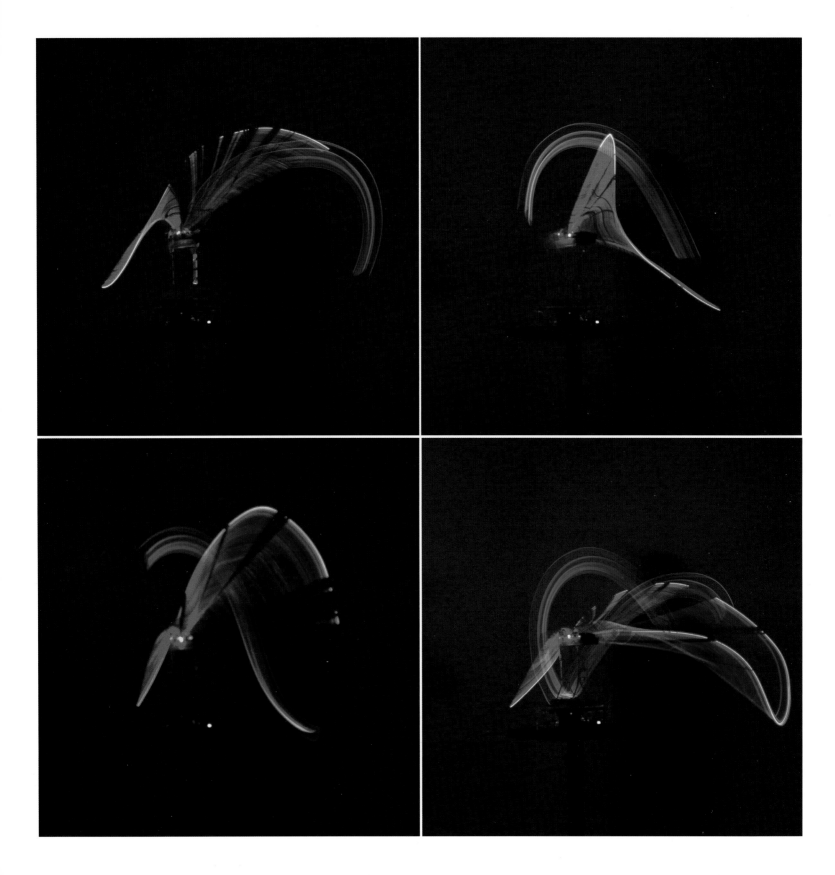

< Inspired by the experimental photography of Gjon Mili, the installation 'Signallers' was built to explore the recording of gestural interactions between a robotic armature and a human arm playing a series of games.

∧ 'Traceries with lights attached to foils' Photograph by Gjon Mili, 1942. Mili records the gestural interaction of two fencers by capturing the movement of light sources attached to the ends of their foils. On close inspection, subtle moments of interaction can be found in these traces.

Restrictions in the reactive model

'User Interface' design has provided usability and a sense of control to the otherwise extremely complex world of digital computation. At the same time it should be noted that these interfaces construct rigid restrictions on how we use technology.

Artist David Rokeby argues that the "computer sets up the illusions that total control is possible. But the crux of this illusion is the fact that the control only functions effectively within the carefully constructed ambiguity vacuum of the computer". (Rokeby, 2003)

One particularly prescriptive model, the WIMP Graphical User Interface or 'Windows, Icons, Menus and Pointing device' conceived by Douglas Englebart in the 1960s and developed in the 1970s at Xerox Parc, has become the ubiquitous model for our daily use of computers at work and in the home. While it has been credited with making the use of computers more accessible to a larger market, it could equally be credited with typifying the homogenisation of human computer interaction.

Today's Operating System GUI's are for the most part identical to GUI's developed in the late 1970s and early 1980s, apart from now being in glorious high resolution 32bit Colour with bouncing icons. As Cybernetician and Software Designer Paul Pangaro humorously suggests, "Most modern software interface designs... do not involve interacting very much at all. They are more like command-line instructions dressed up in drag".(1993)

Underneath the aesthetic surface of current 'interaction design', as it is now fashionably called, is a formula that dates back to the earliest days of 'batch' oriented mechanical punch card technology; a formula of user/master commanding computer/slave rather than of interaction.

Artists and designers investigating novel approaches to engaging with responsive objects and environments have, over the past half century, explored the entire spectrum of sensory and actuation technologies. A driving factor in these works is the dissatisfaction with the rigid limitations of conventional human computer interaction (HCI) approaches.

Creative use of technology in the arts has provided a valuable research and development platform. In dance, for example, motion tracking and gesture recognition using computer vision, mechanical motion capture devices and force sensors (such as accelerometers) have not just enabled new artistic expression, but also revealed the otherwise unexplored potential of these technologies for designing novel interfaces. These developments have unquestionably contributed to the computer gaming industry exploring new gaming paradigms beyond 'button bashing'. Recent examples including Microsoft's computer vision system called 'Natal' and the Nintendo's Wii Controller, offering appealing alternatives to the dated 'joystick' inherited from the Arcade Machines of the 1970s. Clearly there is still space for rethinking the most fundamental elements of how we control and communicate with digital systems, and it is often at the fringes of the creative arts that these new territories are challenged, providing an important testing ground for liberating and extending our relationship with technology in both commercial and artistic endeavours.

Experiments in complexity

In the early 1980s, David Rokeby was an artist whose discontent with the limitations computer interfaces led him to develop 'Very Nervous System' as an attempt to "draw in as much of the universe's complexity into the computer as possible". (Rokeby, 2003)

As he described it, his "interactive environment", built between 1982 and 1990, was, for its time, a sophisticated computer vision system detecting accurate location and movement information that was then interpreted and mapped to a bank of sounds and instruments.

The system constructed by Rokeby was made up of video cameras, image processors, computers, synthesisers and a sound system. He personally developed and mapped out the sounds through his own experimentation in front of the camera and was able to achieve a considerable level of control, much like a musician using his own musical instrument. "That every 'pixel' of the space corresponds to a sound" (Rokeby 1998). In a metaphorical sense, he knew what keys to press.

When 'Very Nervous System' was first presented in Vancouver, Rokeby was surprised by how difficult other people found it to use. Over time, however, people started to play with the space and become aware that the system was reacting to even very subtle gestures and started to build mental maps of the spatialised instrument. The complexity and surprising musical expressions that came out of this system were not of the machine's doing, rather of the complexity of human movement within space.

In an interview, Rokeby described how he wished to create systems of 'inexact control'. "I think that the computer is the result of a fetishization of control and so I like, in my contrary way, to work against that dominant paradigm. Control is over-rated... Or perhaps it is better to say that we need to learn to balance control which is very useful in surgery or driving, with other sorts of engagements with other things and otherness that are looser than control relationships where we allow ourselves to be open, engaged and willing to be surprised. Otherwise life is dead." (Rokeby 2003)

The desire to make artworks that not only surprised the audiences but the artists themselves, became a notable characteristic of mid to late 20th Century time-based art practice. A desire to break free of rigid processes led to aleatoric artworks in Dadaism and Surrealism. At the extreme edges of aleatoric artwork, John Cage, a leading figure of the post-war avant-garde, experimented with computer music using randomisation or chance within parameters defined in the ancient Chinese book I Ching, as a generator for constructing musical scores for performances.

Cage's approach could be argued to be just as rigid algorithmically as traditional reactive systems because the designer of the system (master) commands (slave) to produce a response between parameters that the designer decides. As a result, the randomisation is a constant range of varying values within the boundary values set and hence there is no possibility that something surprising will appear outside of these constraints.

In both Cage's use of randomisation and Rokeby's capture of the complexity of human movement, rigid rules about the processing of input stimuli into output action can be seen to create great variety, but equally we should recognise that these rigid rules build finite barriers that cannot be passed. The weakness of such rigid systems is that the user of these reactive systems is unable to extend or push the system beyond the fixed parameters that the designer pre-choreographs.

Losing of control

Rokeby's installation could be understood to be forcing its inhabitants to adapt their behaviours to meet the rigid configuration of the installation. Rokeby himself describes how his installation began to control his own behaviour. "I saw a videotape of myself moving in the installation. I was moving in a completely unusual and unnatural way, full of jerky tense motions which I found both humorous and distressing,"(1998). His own installation contorted his actions, control was inverted and Rokeby became a slave to suit its uncompromising algorithms.

The Rokeby's intention to find new forms of artistic expression by building systems that capture human gesture in greater resolution is admirable and so too the work of other pioneering artists who've used computer vision, such as Myron Kreugar and Rafael Lozano Hemmer. Sensory data provides rich material for artists to work with. However, the use of sensory technologies that then influence the behaviour of an artwork in some manner don't immediately qualify an artwork as interactive.

Rokeby's 'Very Nervous System' is just one prominent example of an 'interactive installation' that does not involve interacting very much at all. Nevertheless, it is not uncommon in the arts for such work to be described as 'interactive' and Rokeby was awarded the Prix Ars Electronica Award of Distinction for Interactive Art for 'Very Nervous System' in 1991. This only serves to highlight a general confusion within the arts on the clear definition of interactivity.

Redefining interactivity

"By obscuring the distinction between interactive and reactive we lose a potentially fertile conceptual framework"(Haque 2007b). 'Very Nervous System' reacted obediently rather than ever having a life of its own. When people entered and triggered sounds in the space, it was much like a musician activating keys on a keyboard as apposed to a dancer and musician improvising and collaborating a performance together. If the system had the ability to suggest alternative sounds or reposition the arrangement of the sounds spatially of its own accord then perhaps some control would be taken away from the inhabitant.

If this system could then observe how occupants respond to this, it could begin to learn what kinds of arrangements keep people in the space longest and start to collaborate in the creation of new performances and the spatial reconfiguration of sound. This capacity

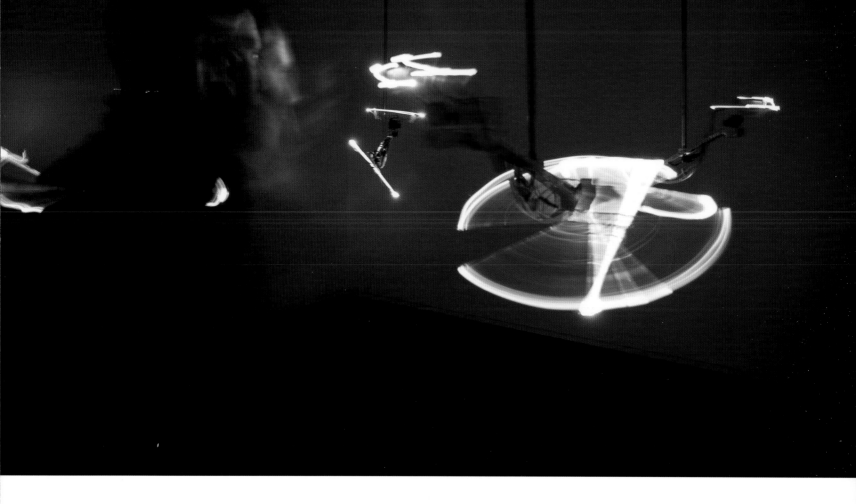

∧ Performative Ecologies,
observing being observed.
Presented in a square
arrangement at 'VIDA'
Exhibition, Madrid, Spain, 2009.

Performative Ecologies,
presented in a linear
arrangement at 'Emergencia'
Exhibition, São Paulo, Brazil, 2008.

to adapt its own behaviour would move the relationship from master/slave towards a more natural conversational relationship with inhabitants.

This conversational model is participatory rather than dictatorial and is a form of social communication that promotes a circularity of interactions, where participants contribute to a shared discourse negotiating their actions and understandings with other participants. Such a model of interaction is most evident in human conversation, but can also be more widely seen in the ecological interactions of our entire natural kingdom.

A conversational model is a different form of communication to that of a network of computers sending packets of data to each other. Conversation, rather than a transmission of signals with definite meaning, is a more creative process of exchange. We use conversation because we can never get inside the head of those we communicate with, so meaning has to be constructed between participants through verbal and non-verbal discourse. "An endless loop of confrontation and disagreement is the process of negotiation: and negotiation involves a process of exchange and potential difference (error) reduction that is both inherently cybernetic and familiarly everyday." (Glanville, 2007)

This leads to the cross-fertilisation of different understandings to form new understandings that are not from either of the participants but rather a construct of their shared interactions. In this way, interaction is not just restricted to the rigid behaviours of reactive systems but is open to forming new understandings and actions. Such a model is therefore productive and open to change beyond the preconceived ideas of individual participants. As an extension of this, if designed artefacts are given the ability to improvise, negotiate and learn themselves, they have the potential, through interaction with other participants, to evolve their own personal behaviours beyond the preconceived notions of their original designer.

Such an evolutionary process achieves the aesthetic desire to design surprising and un-choreographed behaviours in artefacts in which many artists, including Rokeby and Cage, were interested. The difference between these surprising outcomes and those of the rigid noisy algorithms of Cage and Rokeby, is that these are constructed out of the dialogue that occurs in the conversational environment and as a result are contextual to the collaboration of participants rather than generated out of random or pseudo-randomisation.

For designers to engage with this model of participation, some level of autonomy must be built into these artefacts, so that they may make suggestions themselves and make judgments based on their own observations. Reciprocally, I would suggest that for us to become conversational partners with these kinds of systems we must be willing to not just command them but listen and learn from them ourselves.

Certainly you can argue that this relinquishing of control can lead to systems that misbehave or act irrationally, and it is true that by giving systems the ability to make their own suggestions, the capacity for error is inevitable, much like it is in all human beings and animals. You would not want to make an elevator improvises where it stops and opens doors or a life support machine have surprising behaviours, but in the scenarios where we are looking for artefacts that can contextually adapt, collaborate and surprise, sharing of control is a potentially rewarding strategy for all participants.

'Performative Ecologies'
Within the darkened installation space, a dance evolves as a community of autonomous but very sociable robotic sculptures perform with their illuminated tails for inhabitants. Rather than being pre-choreographed, these creatures propose and negotiate with their audience, learning how best to attract and maintain their attention.

Using a genetic algorithm to evolve performances, and facial recognition to assess attention levels (fitness), the individual dancers learn from their successes and failures. As they gain experience, they share their knowledge with the larger ecology, dancing to each other, exchanging their most successful techniques and negotiating future performances collaboratively.

An ecology constructed by both robotic sculptures and human inhabitants, through an intertwining of networks rich in circularities of reciprocal gestures and adaptation. A dance is formed in which individual participants, both human and robotic, operate as performative agents, each acting independently, but continually negotiating their choreography with each other.

The installation's physical composition of four independently responsive sculptures is built from perspex, steel and aluminium. Each one is actuated by servos: two in the 'head', one in their 'tails' and one up at ceiling level, which orientates their body. Each tail has RGB lighting embedded within them so that they can perform the entire wide range of colour and lighting effects. Able to rotate 360 degrees, they each occupy 1.5m in diameter and hang facing their audience at eye height.

It is most often exhibited in near-dark rooms to enhance the brightly illuminated tails, but it has also been presented in daylight when the installation was shown at the Kunsthaus gallery in Graz, Austria. It was strategically positioned on the ground floor of the Gallery looking out at the people walking by on the street. In this setting, the object's contextually adapted to their environment, learning not just how to attract people within the gallery but also out on the street, almost beckoning them to come inside. The vision of the robots was additionally transmitted onto BIX, the Kunsthaus Gallery's large media facade, presenting the activity of the installation out over the city.

The performances are generated from a gene pool of evolving dances functioning in a genetic algorithm (G.A.), which uses facial recognition to assess attention levels and orientation of the audience before and after each performance as a way of assessing and assigning a fitness value to each new choreography. Over time, successful manoeuvres are kept and recombined to produce new performances, while less effective ones are discarded. Mutation in the G.A. fluctuates based on how successful the sculptures become. If they get a lot of attention, mutation levels rise as if they are getting arrogant and as a result become more experimental.

When there are no people around, they turn to each other and teach their most successful performances to each other negotiating new performances together. They take the suggestions of their surrounding partners and compare their gene pool of performances to their partner's suggestions. If they are comparatively similar then they are accepted and replace a chromosome from their own pool. If they are too different they are rejected, as if they dislike the partners dance moves.

Currently, this is done via a wireless network, but it is hoped that in later iterations it will be possible for the sculptures to use their computer vision systems to interpret each other's performances, adding interesting potential for degrees of misunderstandings to occur.

'Colloquy of Mobiles'
In the process of developing 'Performative Ecologies', I made the fortunate discovery of theories and experimental machines of Cybernetician Gordon Pask (1928-1996). Pask provided rigorous terminology for conversation, interaction, environments and participation for artists to use (Haque 2007b). His ongoing contribution to the design of interactive art, architecture and design was in distinguishing the essential features of conversation and the mechanisms by which participants could enter into and continue to converse. Pask himself embodied these conversational mechanisms in a number of computation and theatrical machines that he developed.

In 1968, Pask presented the 'Colloquy of Mobiles', an installation made up of conversational machines at the Cybernetic Serendipity Exhibition, ICA, London. Prior to the exhibition, Pask wrote A comment, a case history and a plan later published in 1971, in which he outlined his belief that: "Man is prone to seek Novelty in his environment and having found a novel situation, to learn how to control it...These propensities are at the root of curiosity and the assimilation of knowledge. They impel man to explore, discover and explain... they lead him into social communication, conversation and other modes of partially co-operative interaction... My contention is that man enjoys performing these jointly innovative and cohesive operations. Together they represent an essentially human and inherently pleasurable mode of activity" (Pask,1971).

His view of conversation as innovative, and pleasurable gave it an aesthetic value that he considered could extend artistic practice and the experience of those who engage with an artwork. Pask presented four key attributes that create 'aesthetically potent environments ', which he described as "environments designed to encourage or foster the type of interaction which is (by hypothesis) pleasurable". The fourth of these points stated that an artwork may "respond to a man, engage him in conversation and adapt its characteristics to the prevailing mode of discourse" (Pask, 1971). With this understanding. Pask's 'Colloquy of Mobiles' was built as a 'socially-orientated' environment. His use of mobiles was intentionally to give the conversation objects formal characteristics 'within the conventions of art'.

Pask recognised that conversation was not exclusively a human ability and showed that it could occur between machines with the capacity to adapt and learn performing as social and conversational environments without the need for human stimulation. With the addition of people entering into this environment, the richness of interactions and relationships could transform and grow into further surprising collaborative performances. Importantly, Pask's Mobiles were not technologically advanced machines by today's standards, yet they had a conceptual sophistication missing in most contemporary so-called interactive art, architecture and design.

Pask's work is not well represented in literature, perhaps through a lack of detailed documentation or perhaps because his work was ahead of its time and not recognised widely enough until much later. Usman Haque and Paul Pangaro are running an on-going project called 'Paskian Environments' to rediscover the work of Pask and reconsider its relevance to the construction of interactive environments. Their detailed analysis of his theoretical constructs and machines are intended to lead to a number of future installations.

From a personal perspective, Pask's models of interaction as conversational and the embodiment of these ideas in machines have been inspirational, providing a useful precedent for interaction design in its truest sense. I believe that if he was still with us today, he would be building machines employing the latest computer vision and advances in machine learning to create interactive systems that could participate in increasingly sophisticated conversations.

Conclusions
Today, time-based design follows a predominantly reactive model. With ever increasing saturation of sensors, processors and actuators in our built environment, commercial products are being produced using reactive and I have argued archaic HCI models that often limit the potential of systems, making them not just slaves to our demands, but us as slaves to their rigid algorithms.

"Now at the beginning of the 21st Century, Pask's Conversation Theory seems particularly important because it suggests how, in the growing field of ubiquitous computing, humans, devices and their shared environments might coexist in a mutually constructive relationship," (Haque 2007b). The potential benefits of 'Conversational Environments' being revisited by a growing number of practicing artists, architects and designers are far-reaching, not just in creative but commercial practice. The role here for artists, architects and designers with an understanding of the conversational model of interaction must be to use and promote this approach to time-based design as a more progressive alternative to the reactive model.

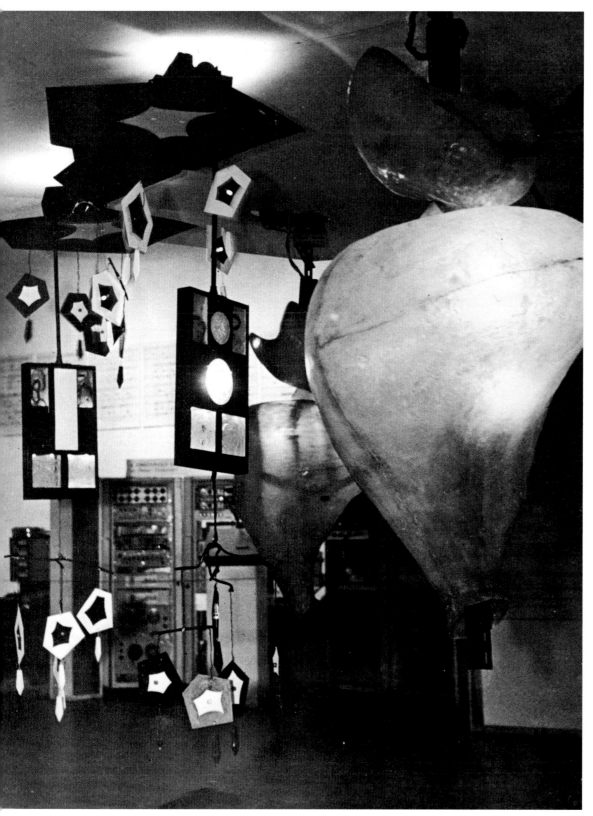

‹ Gordon Pask's 'Colloquy
   of Mobiles', 'Cybernetic
   Serendipity' Exhibition, ICA,
   London, 1968.

References

(S Gage 2002) "Heinz Von Foerster is a Member
of the Viennese Magic Circle" in Spiller N. (Ed.)
Architectural Design: Reflexive Architecture,
Volume 72, Number 3

(R Glanville 2001) "An Intelligent Architecture",
Convergence vol. 7, no 2.

(R Glanville 2007) "Conversation and Design", in
Luppicini, R (ed) *The Handbook of Conversation
Design for Instructional Applications*, Hershey PA,
Idea Group

(U Haque 2007b) "Distinguishing Concepts:
Lexicons of Interactive Art and Architecture"
Bullivant L. (Ed.) *Architectural Design: 4dsocial:
Interactive Design Environments*. Volume 77,
Number 4

(U Haque 2007b) "The Architectural Relevance
of Gordon Pask" In Bullivant L. (Ed.) *Architectural
Design: 4dsocial: Interactive Design Environments*.
Volume 77, Number 4

(PL Pangaro 1993) Pask as Dramaturg, *Systems
Research*, Volume 10 no 3

(G Pask 1961) *An Approach to Cybernetics*,
London, Methuen

(G Pask 1971) "A Comment, A Case History and
A Plan", in Reichardt J (ed.), *Cybernetics, Art and
Ideas*, London, Studio Vista

(D Rokeby 1998) *The Construction of Experience,
Digital Illusion: Entertaining the Future with High
Technology*, Dodsworth, C. (ed.), ACM Press

(D Rokeby 2003) "Very Nervous System and the
Benefit of Inexact Control", Interview by Roberto
Simanowski. www.dichtung-digital.org/2003/1-
Rokeby.htm

SARA SHAFIEI

MAGICIAN'S THEATRE

The design for a Magician's theatre readdresses the sensuality and ornamental richness of the Italian baroque. Notions of magical illusion and geometric anamorphosis generate surgically constructed laser-cut models that describe the functional solution of the circulation, as well as the special complexity of this realm of projections, performances and illusions.

The work attempts to move conventional architectural drawings off the page, from two-dimensional surfaces to three-dimensional constructs, convoluting structural and synthetic design criteria to understand the architecture in its layered assemblage. Within the flesh of anamorphic tectonics, elephants are made to disappear: Houdini's favourite trick.

The Vanishing Elephant:

At the height of his career, Harry Houdini marched to the edge of the stage at the New York Hippodrome and propelled his voice across the footlights to an expectant crowd of 5,200 people, announcing his newest headline-making innovation.

"Lay-deeahs and gintle-menh," he began, holding a finger upright, "perhaps you have all-red-dy heard of the fame and a-comp-lish-ments of my spesh-shel guest!"

The world famous daredevil, escape artist, self-liberator, movie star, publicity genius and mystery performer was, in real life, a little man. On the enormous stage of the hippodrome, he seemed even smaller, but he compensated with an oversized energy, just as he corrected a thick east side of Manhattan accent by over-enunciating each syllable; his words stabbed the back wall of the theatre like a knife. "Allow me to introduce to you, Jennie! The world's only vanishing ell-ee-phant!"

Hiding The Elephant: How Magicians Invented the Impossible (2003) by Jim Steinmeyer

This project attempts to portray how magic and illusion can become an inherent part of architectural design, which foregrounds the engagement of the user in the building. The proposal begins by exploring how Harry Houdini's 'Vanishing Elephant' trick is manifested within Albrecht Dürer's 'Cone of light and vision' to merge showmanship, optics and perspectival illusion.

The resultant building is found in the National Botanical Gardens in Rome, Italy. The building sits at the peak of the site overlooking the gardens. Creating a fluid path leading from the gardens into the theatre, the existing grand stone staircase acts as a foyer and main entrance to the building.

The structure of the building is rooted in excess baroque ornamentation. The laser cutter is harnessed to create detailed pattering on the façade of the building, allowing light to filter through the skin, creating a 'glowing' theatre in the hills, enticing visitors inside. The use of perspectival illusions, such as text and cone anamorphosis, aids in the creation of a landscape of deceptions, whose ornamental tectonics are revealed to the dynamic spectator.

The trick:

'*The spectator makes the picture.*' Marcel Duchamp

Anamorphosis is "a distorted projection or representation of an image on a plane or curved surface, which, when viewed from a certain point, or as reflected from a curved mirror, appears regular and in proportion; a deformation of an image." (Webster's Dictionary)

Anamorphosis can be seen to use perspective constructions to create a 'trick'. The viewer is presented with something that does not make sense when viewed conventionally, and so they must seek out the unconventional viewpoint in order to resolve the 'trick'. Anamorphosis therefore becomes a secret in which the search and discovery of images became an act of magic.

In order to unravel an anamorphic image, the subject's relationship to the object of vision much be altered. As Dan Collins suggests in *Anamorphosis and the Eccentric Observer* (1992): "For the viewer to observe anamorphic image they must become an 'eccentric observer', an observer who is willing to sacrifice a centric vantage point for the possibility of catching the uncanny."

From a traditional point of view, sculpture and architecture implicitly endorse an observer willing to link conventional profiles of an object into a flawless and

> Laser-cut sectional
model of Theatre.
The structure of the building
is rooted in excess baroque
ornamentation. The laser cutter
is harnessed to create detailed
pattering on the facade of the
building, allowing light to filter
through the skin, creating a
'glowing' theatre in the hills,
enticing visitors inside.

‹ Final sectional model of theatre
on site.

⌄ Initial paper model illustrating
materialisation of cones of light
onto an existing stage. The new
design encapsulates Houdini's
Vanishing Elephant.

harmonious progression. There are very few projects that break away from this mould. Borromini's Colonnade in the Palazzo Spada in Rome, Palladio's Teatro Olimpico in Vicenza and the Andrea Pozzo's false vault in Saint Ignatius church in Rome represent the inverse of the norm, as their architecture insists on establishing a hierarchy of views that favour a specific vantage point. This form of design allows the viewer to become part of the process of creating an image, and therefore they become an inherent part of the final product.

As Stephen Gage suggest in *Constructing The User* (2007): "Environments could be constructed out of an array of exquisite objects. These might be the enclosing structures, lighting systems, environmental modulators, routes and passages. The 'observer' in these worlds of natural magic would construct their own understanding and would be delighted in the process of doing this." Environments that allow their user to interact with them make far more interesting pieces of architecture. As Gage states: "An architecture which is founded on illusion has considerable staying power, possibly because it has the concept of an audience imbedded in it. A durable architecture of possibilities may be constructed as an architecture of illusions."

Anamorphosis is used as a tool of illusion in the architectural proposal and allows for the possibility of this outcome. Here, anamorphosis is used on the façade of the theatre. The façade holds the distorted anamorphic image, and the cone (which intersects the facade) becomes the plane, which in turn reveals the true image.

‹ Conical mirror anamorphosis;
  Anamorphic image of Houdini's
  Vanishing Elephant cabinet
  onsite.

› Conical mirror anamorphosis:
  Anamorphic image of interior
  view of auditorium.

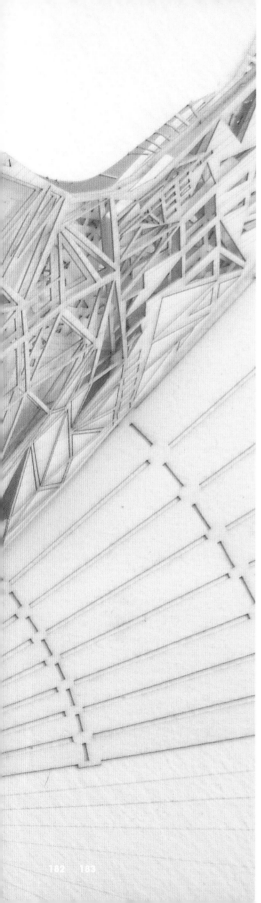

1:20 laser cut detail model of stage and main entrance to theatre. Model is sliced on three sides to reveal interior, exterior and anamorphic cone on the facade of building. The anamorphic cone reflects the words box office.

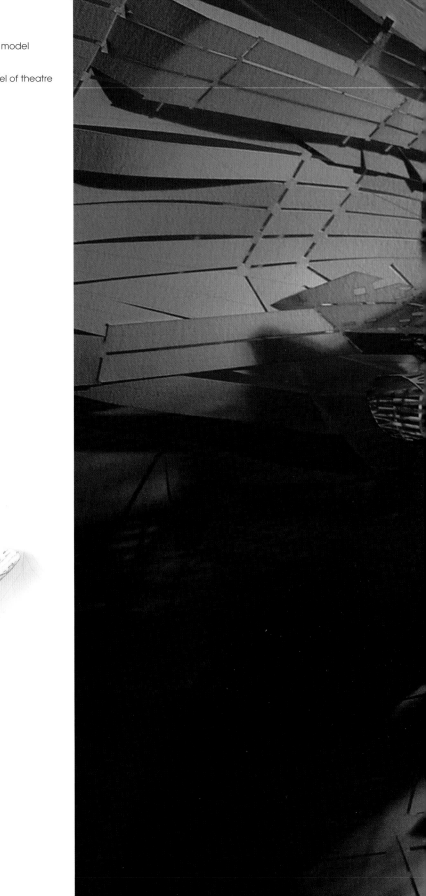

- ⌄ Laser cut sectional model of theatre. 1:100

- › Final laser cut model of theatre on site. 1:100

Ruairi Glynn

Ruairi Glynn is an artist, curator, writer and lecturer in
Interaction Design and Architecture. He teaches at the
Bartlett School of Architecture, University College London
& Centrals Saint Martins College of Art and Design,
University of Arts London. He has been visiting lecturer and
ran workshops on interactive architecture at the Institute
of Digital Art & Technology, UK, the Interactive Institute,
Sweden, the Architectural Association, UK, and Delft
Faculty of Architecture Netherlands.

His personal work has been exhibited internationally
including New York, Sao Paulo, Seoul, Madrid, Vienna
and Los Angeles, winning notable international acclaim
including the Europrix Award for Digital Media, Concurso
Internacional de Arte y Vida Artificial, and Submerge
Innovation Award.

He was curator of 'Interactive Architecture &
Media' Eyebeam Gallery, New York 2007, and 'Gravity,
Pendulums, & Collisions' 'BIX Facade' Kunsthaus,
Graz, Austria 2008, is the founder and editor of
www.interactivearchitecture.org and director of the
Digital Architecture London Conference.

Sara Shafiei

Sara Shafiei graduated from the Bartlett School of
Architecture (UCL), where she received the Sir Banister
Fletcher Bronze Medal, 3D REID Prize, Hamilton Associates
Prize and the TECU International Architecture Award.

Her work delves into the relationship of new
architectural interventions in order to produce a
contemporary style rich in textures, patterns and layers,
mixing baroque influences with the precision of 21st
century modes of making. She has been able to travel
to research her interests further in 2008, through receiving
the British Architecture Foundation Public Space
Travel Award.

She has exhibited in Bogata, Lima, Kassel, Essen,
London and New York. In 2008, she was awarded the
Royal Academy of Arts Summer Exhibition Drawing Prize.

In 2007 Sara co-founded saraben-studio with
Ben Cowd. The award winning office staged their solo
exhibition in 2007. The studio are members of Horhizon, a
network of young designers who collaborate on design
projects and academic workshops across Europe.

Sara is currently teaching diploma and masters at
The Leicester School of Architecture and is a visiting critic
for Cardiff University, The Architectural Association, The
Royal college of Art and the Ecole Speciale D'architecture
Paris, University of Westminster and the Bartlett school
of Architecture.

LIST OF WORKS

Bartlett School of Architecture

UNIVERSITY OF WESTMINSTER

Royal College of Art
Postgraduate Art and Design

Toby Burgess
School: Architectural Association
Tutors: Steve Hardy, Jonas Lundbergtobias

Darren Chan
School: University of Westminster
Tutors: Andrei Martin, Andrew Yau

Gemma Douglas
School: Royal College of Arts
Tutors: Ollie Alsop, Nicola Koller & Gerrard O'Carroll

Tom Dunn
School: Bartlett School of Architecture
Tutors: Bob Sheil, Emmanuel Vercruysse

Adam Nathaniel Furman
School: Architectural Association
Tutors: Natasha Sandmeier, Monia De Marchi

Kostas Grigoriadis, Irene Shamma,
Alexander Robles-Palacio, Pavlos Fereos
School: Architectural Association
Tutor: Theo Spyropoulos

Jordan Hodgson
School: Royal College of Arts
Tutors: Roberto Bottazzi, Tobias Klein

Damjan Iliev
School: University of Westminster
Tutors: Dr. Marjan Colletti, Dr. Marcos Cruz

Yuting Jiang
School: Bartlett School of Architecture
Tutors: Dr. Marjan Colletti, Dr. Marcos Cruz

Julian Jones, Rafael Contreras, Matei Denes,
Diego Ricalde
School: Architectural Association
Tutor: Yusuke Obuchi

Christian Kerrigan
School: Bartlett School of Architecture
Tutors: Neil Spiller, Phil Watson

Kenny Kinugasa-Tsui
School: Bartlett School of Architecture
Tutors: Dr. Marjan Colletti, Dr. Marcos Cruz

Tobias Klein
Synthetic Syncretism
School: Bartlett School of Architecture
Tutors: Dr. Marjan Colletti, Shaun Murray
Soft Immortality
Tutors: Neil Spiller, Phil Watson

Ric Lipson
School: Bartlett School of Architecture
Tutors: Bob Sheil, Emmanuel Vercruysse

Tetsuro Nagata
School: Bartlett School of Architecture
Tutors: Stephen Gage, Phil Ayres, Richard Roberts

Marilena Skavara
School: Bartlett School of Architecture
Tutors: Ruairi Glynn, Sean Hanna, Alasdair Turner

Tarek Shamma
School: Architectural Association
Tutors: Natasha Sandmeier, Monia DeMarchi

Matthew Shaw
School: Bartlett School of Architecture
Tutors: Bob Sheil, Emmanuel Vercruysse

Nicholas Szczepaniak
School: University of Westminster
Tutors: Susanne Isa, Sacha Leong, Markus
Seifermann

Charlotte Thomas
School: Architectural Association
Tutors: Anne Save de Beaurecueil, Franklin Lee

Patrick Usborne
School: Architectural Association
Tutors: Chris Lee, Sam Jacoby

Johan Voordouw
School: Bartlett School of Architecture
Tutors: Dr. Marjan Colletti, Dr. Marcos Cruz

Michael Wihart
School: Bartlett School of Architecture
Tutors: Phil Watson, Neil Spiller, Marcos Cruz

Amanda Levete Architects
Corian Lounge

AL_A Design Team
Amanda Levete, Alvin Huang, Alex Bulygin,
Chiara Ferrari, Filippo Previtali
Project Leader: Bruce Davison

Collaborators
Margaritelli / Listone Giordano®, Isometrix Lighting
Design, Nemo divisione luci di Cassina, molo,
Hasenkopf, Esarc Hi-tech

Amanda Levete Architects
Spencer Dock Bridge

Client
Dublin Docklands Development Authority, Railway
Procurement Agency

Location
Dublin

Programme
Bridge for vehicles, tram and pedestrians
Contract Value: £4.5 million

AL_A Team
Amanda Levete, Peter Feldman, Jordy Fu, Alvin
Huang, Theo Sarantoglou
Project Architect: Alan Dempsey
Photography: Gidon Fuehrer

Structural Engineers
Arup

marcosandmarjan
75ª Feira do Livro de Lisboa
Project for the 75th Lisbon Book Fair, 2005

Client
Câmara Municipal de Lisboa, EGEAC

Team
Design: marcosandmarjan
Collaborators: João Albuquerque, Shui Liu,
Marco Sacci
Associate Architects: Guedes & Viinikainen
Associate Engineer: Francisco Bernardo—A400
Graphic Design: Barbara Says
Laser Cutting: Lasindústria
Construction: Contubos

Contrstruction cost: 500.000.00 Euros
Programme: General layout of Book Fair,
Cafeteria, Auditorium, Outside Esplanade,
Information Pavilion
Total construction area: 1000m²

----

marcosandmarjan
Nurbster I

Installation for Unit 20
Bartfest 04—Slade School of Art UCL, London UK
(July 2004)
Young British Architecture—Fragner Gallery,
Prague Czech Republic (Oct–Dec 2004)

Team
Design: marcosandmarjan with Unit 20
Assembling: Students of Unit 20
Manufacturing: Zone Creations

Sponsor
The Great Britain Sasakawa Foundation

marcosandmarjan
Nurbster IV—Splinewall

Installation done during the Feng Jia University &
Bartlett School of Architecture Digital Architecture
Design Workshop, Taichung Taiwan

Team
Design / Tutors: marcosandmarjan
Workshop Organisers: Simon Shu, Beatrice Hsien,
(Trudi Ko)
Students:Tze-Chun Wei (Jim), Wen-Ting Chang
(Wendy), Chi-Chih Mao (Chi Chi), Po-Chuan Chen
(Paul), Fang-Wei Tsao, Li-Wu Wang (Wu), Hsueh-
Chan Yang (Akira), Ping-Hsun Li (Bob), Chun Wan,
Ping-Chen Liu (Benson), Chih-Chien Liao (Ray),
Chun-Hung Chen, Meng-Hung Cheng (Sam),
Tsung-Yu Tsai, Tung-Chieh Su (Victor), Shu-Min Fu
(Sumi), Pin-Chi Yu (Erik), Yao-Hui Huang (Grace),
Chen-An Pan (Pan), Chien-Min Chen (Steven),
Kuo-Pang Hsiao (Shawn), Ke-Hsiu Wu (Louis), Wei-Ti
Huang (Jason), Yu Hsuan Huang (Fred), Chun-
Teng Li (Ivy), Tze Hau Chen (Pika Chen)
Laser Cutting: Chun-Sheng Industry Limited
Company, Taichung Taiwan
Alan Dempsey & Alvin Huang

(C)Space Drl10 Pavilion

Architects
Alan Dempsey and Alvin Huang

Consultants
Structural Engineers: Adams Kara Taylor

Sponsors
Rieder Beton, Zaha Hadid Architects, Adams Kara
Taylor, Buro Happold, Innova Construction, DHA
designs

Organisers
Yusuke Obuchi, Patrik Schumache

Client
Architectural Association, Design Research Lab

PROJECT DETAILS

ACKNOWL

On behalf of all of us, we'd like to thank all the contributors: Neil Spiller, David Greene, Samantha Hardingham, Amanda Levete Architects, Julien De Smedt architects, Bruce Davison, Sam McElhinney, Usman Haque, Bob Sheil of sixteen*(makers), marcosandmarjan, Alvin Huang, Plasma Studio, Philip Beesley, Mette Ramsgard Thomsen, Toby Burgess, Darren Chan, Gemma Douglas, Tom Dunn, Adam Nathaniel Furman, Kostas Grigoriadis, Irene Shamma, Alexander Robles-Palacio, Pavlos Fereos, Jordan Hodgson, Damjan Iliev, Yuting Jiang, Julian Jones, Rafael Contreras, Matei Denes, Diego Ricalde, Christian Kerrigan, Kenny Kinugasa-Tsui, Tobias Klein, Ric Lipson, Tetsuro Nagata, Marilena Skavara, Tarek Shamma, Matthew Shaw, Nicholas Szczepaniak, Charlotte Thomas, Patrick Usborne, Johan Voordouw, Michael Wihart, Andy Usher, Dan Farmer, Declan Shaw, Sam Walker, Subomi Fapohunda, Guy Woodhouse, Elle Lakin, Abi Abdolwahabi, Collyn Ahart Chipperfield and Richard Roberts.

A special thank you to Arup Phase 2 Gallery, the Architectural Association, Bartlett School of Architecture, University of Westminster and Royal College of Art for their generous support.

Ruairi Glynn
There are too many people to thank in person but I must begin by saying I have a wonderful generous family who have given me more love and support than I could ever ask for. A big thank you to my colleagues at the Bartlett, especially to Stephen, thank you for your endless advice, assistance and enthusiasm. Jennifer, thank you for the opportunity, and thank you Phase 2 Gallery for hosting the Digital Hinterlands exhibition. Collyn, thank you for teaching me to just go out there and get it. And finally to the team, Joanna, your eagle eye, your lyrical turn of phrase and your endless optimism have kept us going in the early hours. To my lifelong friend Emily, I never doubted you'd make a beautiful book but this is more than I ever expected. Sara, you're a star. What a journey we've had through the hinterlands. We'll have to go for another wander soon.

Sara Shafiei
Although it is author's name that appears on the cover of the book, and therefore it is she who takes the plaudits, this book would not be possible without the efforts of Emily Chicken. Thank you Emily for your imagination, creativity and most importantly your friendship. I would like to thank the many people who saw me through this book; to all those who provided support, wrote, read, offered comments, provided their amazing work and edited—Joanna Lee you have been great. To my fellow author Ruairi Glynn—we did it against all the odds. Thank you to the Bartlett School of Architecture for jumpstarting my passion for Architecture.

To Johan Voordouw and the rest of the farmers, I have several amazing friends who managed to put up with me through the course of this book, which is an accomplishment in itself.

Lastly a special thank you to my family for their love, encouragement, support and belief. This book is every bit your accomplishment as it is mine.

Emily Chicken
Firstly I would like to say a special thank you to Anthony Michael, for his valuable lesson in self belief. To Sara Shafiei, for her enthusiasm, encouragement and support from day one. To Ruairi Glynn for his spirit, energy and friendship. To Joanna Lee for her brilliant editing. Thanks to Jess Jenkins at Butler Tanner & Dennis. And finally a big thanks to the mum and dad, for their love, support, food parcels and good counsel.

EDGEMENTS